The Eugenic Assault on America

Scenes in Red, White, and Black

J. David Smith

George Mason University Press
Fairfax, Virginia

Copyright © 1993 by
George Mason University Press
4400 University Drive
Fairfax, VA 22030

Distributed by
National Book Network

4720 Boston Way
Lanham, MD 20706

3 Henrietta Street
London WC2E 8LU England

Library of Congress Cataloging-in-Publication Data

Smith, J. David, 1944–
The eugenic assault on America : scenes in red, white, and black /
J. David Smith.
p.   cm.
Includes index.
1. United States—Race relations.   2. Eugenics—United
States—History.   I. Title.
E184.A1S655   1992   305.8'00973—dc20   92–19230 CIP

ISBN 0–913969–53–2 (cloth : alk. paper)

 The paper used in this publication meets the minimum requirements of
American National Standard for Information Sciences—Permanence
of Paper for Printed Library Materials, ANSI Z39.48–1984.

TO THE INDIAN
PEOPLE OF AMHERST COUNTY.

May you find peace
and justice
for
yourselves,
your ancestors,
and your children

Acknowledgments

My first expression of thanks for help with this book goes, as always, to Joyce Smith. She and our children, Lincoln, Allison and Sallie, give me my greatest happiness in life. Their understanding and love make my work possible.

My colleagues, Ed Polloway, Rosel Schewel, Pete Warren, and Ken West, have encouraged my efforts for most of my academic career. I am deeply appreciative of the friendship and wisdom they have shared with me across the years.

I was given valuable and kind assistance while doing research for this book at both the Alderman Library at the University of Virginia, and at the American Philosophical Society Library in Philadelphia. The staff of the Lynchburg College Library was also very helpful to me.

Lynchburg College granted me a sabbatical leave and provided some early financial assistance for my work on this project through the Faculty Committee on Research and Development. These I received as symbols of both confidence and validation. This book would not have become a reality without the support of the Virginia Foundation for the Humanities and Public Policy. As a Resident Fellow at the Foundation's Center I was enabled to do most of the research that resulted in these pages.

Finally, I am glad to be associated with James Fisher of George Mason University Press. His belief in the importance of the message of this book has earned my respect and gratitude.

The Eugenic Assault on America: Scenes in Red, White, and Black

Table of Contents

Acknowledgements v

Preface ix

Chapter One   Eugenics, Nazis and Poor White Trash 1

Chapter Two   Earnest Cox, John Powell, and the
                  Anglo-Saxon Clubs of America 13

Chapter Three   John Powell and Marcus Garvey—The
                  Peculiar Alliance 23

Chapter Four   John Powell, Hampton Institute and the
                  Issue of Racial Equality 37

Chapter Five   W.A. Plecker, Vital Statistics and the
                  Color Line 59

Chapter Six   Dr. Plecker's War on the Indians 71

Chapter Seven   Human Beings as Mongrels, a Eugenic
                  Tragedy 83

Chapter Eight   Documentary Genocide and the Indians
                  of Amherst 89

Chapter Nine   The Monacan Indians of Virginia 101

Chapter Ten   Eugenics as Genocide 109

Index   117

Preface

One of the most vivid memories I have from my childhood is of a trip to Alabama with my parents when I was seven. The trip was for a visit with my mother's family in Montgomery. This was my second rail pilgrimage from Virginia to Alabama. The first was when my brother Carl was an infant and I was four. I have no recall at all of that visit. The second time, probably because of their vivid recollection of having traveled with me as a four year old, my parents decided to leave Carl, now that age, at home in Roanoke with relatives. I remember, and relish even now, the excitement of sleeping in the Pullman car, eating in the dining car, and having the conductor acknowledge the special status bestowed on us by the free pass my father had because he worked as a machinist in the Norfolk and Western Shops. I even had a chance to ride with the engineer for a few precious minutes. I remember so clearly changing trains in Birmingham, the colossus of the passenger station there and riding a new coach the last leg into Montgomery. A vendor passed through the car selling sandwiches and snacks from a large metal box. The image of the cardboard cone of shelled peanuts my mother bought and shared has remained with me now for almost four decades.

Arriving in Montgomery on that summer night was a sleepy blur for a me as a seven year old. I remember only that my Uncle Ray picked us up in a big, black, boat of a car. A quick stop at my grandmother's house, it was late, and then on to Uncle Ray's house; something to eat and to bed.

The next morning was devoted to a real visit with my grandmother and a stop at the firehouse where my uncle worked. Wearing his fireman's hat, ringing the bell on the hook and ladder truck, and blowing the siren for just a second—these are the sorts of things that childhood memories are supposed to be made of. That afternoon, however, was to grant me another kind of memory, a memory which would echo through the rest of my life.

My mother had often talked with me about a woman she called Aunt Celie. Aunt Celie was not a relative. I knew she was a black woman who had been very kind to my mother when she was a child. I heard many times the description of how Celie brushed my mother's hair and told her stories of her own childhood. My mother also frequently recounted for me the fact that Aunt Celie had been a slave when she was a very little girl. Somehow, however, this had not found a special register in my mind and had made no particular impression on me.

On our first afternoon in Montgomery we went to Aunt Celie's home. My perceptions of her, of my mother and of human relationships were changed profoundly as a result of that visit. When we drove up to Aunt Celie's house in Uncle Ray's Buick my mother could barely wait to get out of the car. Her feet were hardly on the sidewalk when she was met by squeals of laughter and delight from Celie and her daughter, Agnes. Soon my mother was squealing also. There were lots of hugs all around and repeatedly I heard an ancient thin voice crying, "My baby, my baby." Before I realized what was happening I was out of the Buick myself and unexpectedly in the embrace of Aunt Celie. She was the oldest person I had ever touched. She squeezed me to her bony and wrinkled body. She was immaculately groomed and she wore a starched white apron over her black Sunday dress. Aunt Celie smelled of talcum powder and her bare hands felt like fine leather gloves. Soon Agnes joined in the hugging and the two of them alternated with choruses of "Its Joyce's boy, its Baby's boy!" I felt absolutely overwhelmed. I also felt like a celebrity.

Soon we were inside the house. Other people, young and old, male and female, all black, moved self consciously in and out of the living room where we sat with Aunt Celie and Agnes. My impression was that all of these people were being headquartered in the kitchen and that each person was assigned his or her turn to come out and be introduced. There were lots of "Growin' like a weed's," "Hasn't changed a bit's" and "Law's me!" I was stunned by it all. Never before had I been so physically close to so many black people. I had just been smothered with embraces from two black women out on the sidewalk and now I was sitting in their home being introduced to what seemed like an army of other black people appearing from their kitchen.

As I remember it, Agnes had a deep rich voice and she was soon insisting that we must all have a "little something" to eat. Almost immediately, it seemed to me, the army of people, now all introduced, were streaming from the kitchen with coffee, cake and lemonade. The cake was cut in thick slices. It was a marble cake, apparently a special treat prepared for my mother. It was served first to her, then my father, uncle, and grandmother; then Agnes brought a piece of cake, a big piece, for me.

I sat silent, confused and afraid with the cake, plate, napkin and fork balanced on my lap. It seemed to me that everyone in the room was watching and waiting for me to take a bite of the cake. I could not move. I felt frozen. I knew that I couldn't lift the cake to eat it and I was frightened that if the plate started to slide off my lap I wouldn't be able to move my hand to stop it. "Take just a bite," "Try a little bit," "Taste Celie's cake," my mother and everyone else in the room seemed to be urging me, cajoling me. I couldn't eat the cake! The moment passed, the embarrassment waned, and the conversation moved on to other things. Later my mother quizzed me about the cake. I couldn't tell her why I wouldn't eat it, I honestly did not know myself. It took many years before I was able to reflect on my memory of that visit with Aunt Celie and decipher what it must have meant in my seven year old grasp of the world of people and relationships.

I did not eat the cake because it was made and served by "colored people." I'm sure that is the correct word to use in describing my sense of the people who were trying so hard to be kind and hospitable to me. The people to whom I could not respond were "colored." I'm certain that is the way I was thinking of Aunt Celie, Agnes and the others that day. My parents would not have used the word "nigger" as I was growing up. While they were certainly products of the southern culture of their own upbringing, they would not have used that word with their children. That word would not have been part of my vocabulary or of my way of thinking about people in 1952. No, I'm sure that "colored" would have been the word in my mind. I had not been taught to hate but some-how I knew that there were cautions and limits necessary when dealing with colored people.

The song from *South Pacific* asserts that children must be "carefully taught" to hate and discriminate. I disagree, I think that prejudice is informally caught rather than formally taught. I think that by the time I was seven years old I had caught the belief from my social environment that black people were not to be touched or trusted. I somehow knew that eating with black people was not a good thing. I think that I had already learned a sense of race and an ethic of racial separation. I cannot recall ever being taught them but I know I had learned those lessons.

But what of my mother? Certainly she knew these things but yet I had seen her allow herself to be embraced like a little girl by Aunt Celie and Agnes. Even more disturbing, she had returned their hugs with enthusiasm and obvious deep affection. She had not only eaten the marble cake, she had tried to persuade me to do the same. It didn't make sense. I was soon relishing my other adventures in Montgomery, however, and remembering with pride having sat behind the wheel of the hook and ladder truck at Uncle Ray's fire-house. The memories of marble cake and Aunt Celie soon settled several layers below my consciousness.

In 1952 racial segregation in public schools was still the norm by law or practice in most parts of the United States. Racial separation in most areas of social life was an enforced standard. Brown v. Board of Education was still only being formulated in Topeka. Freedom rides and lunchcounter protests were as yet undreamed expressions of the yearning for civil rights and personal dignity among America's black people. In Montgomery where I rode the streets in my uncle's shiny black Buick, Rosa Parks was still riding on the back-seat of the bus or standing in its crowded aisle while seats at the front remained unfilled. The bus boycott that would occur in a few years there was as yet unthinkable. Martin Luther King, Jr. was an obscure young preacher.

Over the next twenty years and more my memories of Aunt Celie were called up by events that stimulated once again the puzzling contradiction: Celie loved and was loved deeply by my mother. My mother respected and trusted her. Yet I had learned that the right thing to do was to distance myself from people like her. How could it be that this woman evoked such behavior from my own mother? I recalled Aunt Celie throughout the events of the civil rights movement. I thought of her as I watched news reports of young black men and women being knocked to the ground with firehoses. I remembered her as I watched black boys and girls being cursed by hate filled white adults as they entered segregated public schools. I saw her features in the faces of hundreds of elderly black people during my two years in the Peace Corps. Recognizing Aunt Celie's capacity for love and remembering my immature rejection of her has served as a challenge for growth and change throughout much of my life. I am deeply in her debt.

As I mentioned earlier, my mother told Carl and I stories of Aunt Celie before I met her in Montgomery. She told the stories for years afterward. The stories were always the same. My grandmother ran a small neighborhood grocery in Montgomery. She, my mother and my uncles lived behind the store. The store had no name, it was "nothing fancy." There was no electricity in the store and no indoor plumbing. They sold bologna, bread, crackers, beans, sugar and other things that were considered staples at the time. Kerosene lamps were used for lighting and clothes were washed in a tub with a scrub board. My mother washed clothes in the mornings before going to school and ironed using a charcoal heated iron. She often talked of wearing clothes that other people handed down to her. She explained that, "there was a woman who Mama bought candy from for the store who had a girl a little older than me and she would bring me clothes."

Celie often came to their home behind the store. She brought a wooden box with her to sit on, she refused to sit on their furniture. My mother would sit on the floor; Celie sat on the box, brushed her hair and told stories of her childhood in slavery. Aunt Celie and her mother were separated when she was very small. They were sold to different slaveholders. Celie cried with fear and anguish when she was torn away from her mother. Her new "mistress" gave her a little perfume bottle to play with in an effort to comfort her. She stayed with this family as a slave until she was emancipated a few years later. She told my mother that her "mistress" was "good" to her. Aunt Celie treasured the perfume bottle for most of her life. She treasured it but she treasured my mother more. She gave it to her "baby" as a gift of love.

I always assumed that Aunt Celie was hired by my grandmother to care for my mother. My grandmother raised four children without the help of a husband. I believed that Celie was probably paid to come in during times when my grandmother was most busy with the store. I must admit that there have been times when I have spoken reluctantly of Aunt Celie with other people because I thought her story would sound too much like a "kindly black mammy" tale about the woman who was hired to raise my mother, and what a loyal and loving "servant" she had been. A late night conversation in the fall of 1989, however, added a new dimension to my understanding of the relationship between Aunt Celie and my mother. Aunt Celie was not hired to care for my mother. She was instead a genuine friend and a kind neighbor who was in no sense employed to care. My grandmother's store was in a "colored" section of Montgomery. Most of her customers were black people. When my grandmother went into the labor of my mother's birth she went to the back of the store to her bed. She sent one of my uncles for help. The local doctor could not be found and so she asked for Celie whom by then she had known for some time. Celie came and, "before Dr. Bickerstaff could be found," delivered my mother. For the rest of her life she called my mother her baby or simply "Baby." It was a just claim. She literally brought my mother into the world.

Celie visited often with my mother in her home behind the store. As I said earlier, on these visits she lovingly combed my mother's hair and told her the stories of her life which have remained with her to this day. My mother also visited in Celie's home frequently. She remembers that Celie had a stereoscope, the antique forerunner of what some us knew in childhood as a Viewmaster. She would sit for hours and look at cardboard pictures of dramatic scenes and faraway places. They talked, looked at the pictures through the stereoscope, and ate fresh figs from the tree in Aunt Celie's backyard. These were wonderful times for my mother and she still becomes radiant when she describes them.

Prejudice is a form of mental illness, I'm convinced of it. Unfortunately it is often a form of shared mania that results in great hurt to the subjects of its madness. Most people with other forms of mental illness are dangerous only to themselves. Prejudice is different. Its primary symptom is hatred of others, and those who are hated are at high risk for being hurt. The irrationality of hatred for others because of their race, nationality, religion, gender, social class or other characteristic can become all consuming. That irrationality has proven itself repeatedly to be resistant to all reason and evidence contrary to its poisoned convictions.

Prejudice, however, has often been elevated and dignified by powerful and influential people who have supported it in the name of reason and have advanced it in the name of science. This book is about scientific assaults on people because of their social class or racial identity. It is about laws and practices which have been aimed at controlling the lives of people deemed inferior because of race or class. It is about claims made for a scientific basis for those laws and practices. In that sense it will illustrate that the illness of prejudicial thought can infect the intellect at what we consider its highest levels and in what we think of as its purest forms. It will give glimpses of the lives of people in law, medicine, science and human services who were convinced that they had the right and responsibility to intervene in powerful and intimate ways in the lives of other people for "their own good" and for the protection of society. It will also give glimpses into the lives of those who were hurt by what was done to them in the name of scientific, medical or political necessity. I hope that it will serve as well as a reminder and a warning to all of us who face a future which is sure to be even more socially complex, and confusing, than our past. Confusion and complexity should not seduce us to engage in simple and expedient actions which rob others of their liberty and dignity. Prejudice must be struggled against continually. I don't think that you can simply overcome a "bad case" of it or that you can inoculate a child for life against ever "catching" it. It is all around us and I believe that the challenge is to examine each day the assumptions that we make about other people and the fears we harbor of people because of the way they look, speak, worship or otherwise live their lives. Just when you think you have overcome a prejudicial view you find yourself on one of those dark, lonely streets of life and the complexion of the stranger coming toward you makes a difference in the degree of your discomfort.

In a world filled with negative, and sometimes evil, abstractions about people I have found comfort and reassurance in concrete human interactions. My relationships with people who are handicapped has taught me much about dignity in human life. Some of my most profound lessons about freedom have come from knowing people who are mentally retarded and who were needlessly institutionalized. When I am tempted to allow race to become something negative in my thinking I remember Aunt Celie. I recall her embracing my mother on the sidewalk as I watched in Montgomery that afternoon in 1952 and I imagine the day years before when she gently bathed a newborn with love.

Several times during the last few years I asked my mother about the perfume bottle. I remember seeing it as a child and the image I have is of a small glass vial with a metal filigree covering. Each time I have asked about it she has replied evasively that it is "put away somewhere" and that she will try to find it sometime before my next visit. Somehow the next time I ask it has slipped her mind and it is just too late or she is too busy to look for it just then. I suspect that the bottle is wrapped carefully in flannel cloth scraps and put in a box that once held Christmas cards. I imagine it has been placed safely under rarely used things in a dresser drawer. I also suspect that it has become too precious to share when the house is filled with activity and grandchildren. I understand. I have the memories. That is all that matters.

JDS, 1992

CHAPTER ONE:

Eugenics, Nazis and Poor White Trash

Even before the publication of Charles Darwin's *The Origin of Species* in 1859, the philosopher Herbert Spencer had developed the basic tenets of his own theory of evolution. The most important concept which Spencer gained from Darwin's theory was that of the specific mechanism for the achievement of biological variation, the mechanism of natural selection. It was Spencer, however, who coined two of the terms most commonly associated with the idea of evolution, "the struggle for existence" and "the survival of the fittest."

According to Spencer, the quality of human stock, just as with the fitness of other species, improves slowly through the process of evolution and cannot be changed for the better by any other means. In the primitive human condition, argued Spencer, people necessarily resort to violence and warfare for survival. Warfare, from this perspective, has the positive effect of killing off inferior races, thus promoting the survival and reproduction of superior human strains. As mankind develops complex societies, argued Spencer, the conflicts among people became more economic than military. He cautioned, therefore, that civilized societies must be careful not to foster the survival of the unfit by interfering with seemingly harsh, but essential, economic realities.

Thus, Spencer was opposed to public education. He believed that free public schools would not ultimately improve society but, on the contrary, would pave the way to its degeneration. People should be required to pay for the schooling of their children if they wanted to have them educated. Otherwise the survival advantages of education would be given to the poor whom he felt were inferior as evidenced by their poverty. He opposed sanitation laws, efforts to license doctors and nurses, and compulsory vaccination. He felt that people who were not intelligent enough to find and afford proper medical care ought to be left to suffer the consequences of their intellectual inferiority. In the ideal society, according to Spencer, there would be no social intervention, no regulation of industry, no welfare programs for the poor, nothing which would impede natural selection.

It is not surprising to see that Spencer applied his ideas on human evolution to specific racial groups. He attributed failures and successes among nations to the qualities of their races and the degree of their intermixture of

1

races. Intermarriage between races should be positively forbidden declared Spencer. It is not a question of social philosophy, he said, it is at root a question of biology. Animal breeders had long known, according to this point of view, that the intermixture of stocks leads to degeneration of the resulting breeds. The claimed inferiority of Eurasian people in India and so-called "half-breeds" in America was thus used as an illustration of the negative biological and social effects of race mixing.

In 1883, Francis Galton, a cousin of Charles Darwin, introduced the term "eugenics" in England. He used this word to designate what he proposed as a new science. It was to be the science of "race improvement." An early eugenic goal of Galton and his followers was to promote the use of selective marriage practices in order to eliminate hereditary disorders. Soon, however, eugenic policy was expanded to include the advocacy of compulsory sexual sterilization of people who were considered to be bearers of undesirable physical, intellectual or social traits. Eugenic arguments were also used to advance the practice of institutionalizing people who were considered to be socially or intellectually inferior.

Eugenics had important implications for racial groups and for social classes. From the inception of this new "science" Galton was convinced that there were definite grades of people within each race and that these grades were determined by fixed hereditary realities. He also held that were unalterable grades of the races themselves, some being much more highly evolved than others. He argued that the best classes of people within the Caucasian race were not producing enough children whereas the inferior classes were producing too many offspring. A clear implication was that the upper classes must be encouraged to have more children and that the lower classes must somehow be compelled to have fewer.

Many eugenicists viewed racial inequality as a prime demonstration of the natural order, as an example of the truth of social evolution, of what came to be called social Darwinism. Just as it was the poor heredity of poor classes which kept them poor, so black people had been enslaved earlier because they were actually inferior to the white race which enslaved them, and they were still subjugated socially and economically in fact for the same reason. Far from feeling responsibility or remorse at the near extinction of American Indians, eugenic observers posited that this was the necessary evolutionary process for yielding the land of North America over to superior European stock. When eugenic thought was interpreted into theological terms it portrayed the elimination or subjugation of inferior races as the will of God at work in the world.

The most powerful of the devices employed by eugenicists in advancing their race and class arguments were the family degeneracy studies. These studies typically involved genealogical research on family trees. Inevitably they would yield results indicating that a given negative trait or weakness had been present in all traceable generations of a group of people or had been reoccurring in the ancestors of a particular individual. The conclusion drawn from these results was, of course, that many physical, sociological and psychological problems are hereditary in nature and must be dealt with through aggressive means of social, political and medical control.

Of the family degeneracy studies one of the earliest, most powerful and most influential was reported by Henry Goddard in his book *The Kallikak Family: A Study in the Heredity of Feeble-Mindedness* which was published in 1912. It was that study, its genesis, and its legacy that was the concern of my book *Minds Made Feeble* which was published in 1985.

Goddard, who directed the research laboratory of the Training School at Vineland, New Jersey, published his account of a family that had come to his attention in the course of investigating the role of heredity in mental retardation. The study of this family tree had begun with a young woman who was a resident of the Vineland institution, Deborah Kallikak, who was considered to be feebleminded. More specifically, she had been classified as a "moron," a designation that Goddard had coined from a Greek work meaning foolish. This label came to be widely assigned to people who were considered to be "high grade defectives," those who were not retarded seriously enough to be obvious to the casual observer and who had not been diagnosed as being brain damaged by disease or injury. Morons were characterized as being intellectually dull, socially inadequate and morally deficient. From the beginning of his research Goddard was inclined to believe that these traits were hereditary in origin. He was definitely of the opinion that reproduction among these people posed a threat to social order and the advancement of civilization.

Deborah, who had been born in an almshouse, was admitted to the Vineland Training School for Feeble-Minded Girls and Boys at the age of eight. She was almost twenty-three when the study was published. The name Deborah and the family name Kallikak which she, her relatives and ancestors were given are pseudonyms. Goddard seems to have enjoyed inventing terms, he composed Kallikak from the Greek words kallos (beautiful) and kakos (bad). He used this composite as a symbol of the two hereditary influences which he believed had resulted in Deborah's moronity. A good, or beautiful, hereditary strain in her background had been tainted by a bad genetic seed leading to her inferior intellect. Although the names are fictitious, Goddard emphasized that the "present study of the Kallikak family is a genuine story of real people."

In fact it was not a genuine story at all and the way the people in the study were presented was not real. After searching for and discovering the real family name I conducted my own research on the Kallikaks through census figures, legal records, genealogical information and historical documents. Work at the National Archives, the Library of Congress and in courthouses in New Jersey resulted in a steady unveiling of the Kallikaks, they were really there! More importantly, however, they were there with a difference. The Kallikaks that I found differed greatly from the Kallikaks that Goddard had described. Yes, they were the same individuals, but what the records told me was true of them was often contrary to what Goddard's book had portrayed.

The story of the disfavored Kallikaks, those claimed to have been the bearers of the "bad seed," was not free of troubles and human frailties. The family did have its share of illegitimate children, drunkards, "ne'er-do-well," and the other skeletons that have a way of jumping out of genealogical closets. But so do most families, particularly those who have been faced with poverty, lack of education, and scarce resources for dealing with social change. But the family also had its strengths and successes. The tragedy of the disfavored Kallikaks is that their story was distorted to fit an expectation. They were perceived in a way that allowed only their weaknesses and failures to emerge. Their story was first interpreted according to a powerful myth, and then used to bolster further that same myth. The myth was that of eugenics. All the "bad" Kallikaks were bad because "it ran in the family," according to that myth, and that pseudoscientific legacy would remain unchanged for decades. Even today, in convoluted forms. it continues to have a social and political impact. Its message is simple, yet powerful. That message is that ignorance, poverty, and social pathology are in the blood—in the seed. It is not the environment in which people are born and develop that makes the critical difference in human lives. People are born either favored or beyond help. Social programs, "wars on poverty," and compensatory education are futile and wasteful.

While I was doing research on the Kallikaks in New Jersey during the late winter of 1983–1984, a local newspaper carried two articles on a young woman from the area who had distinguished herself academically and through extracurricular activities at a respected midwestern college. She was an honor student and had been recognized for her artistic talent. This outstanding young person is the great, great, great granddaughter of the Kallikak who Goddard claimed mated with "bad blood"—she is the most recent flowering of the bad seed!

The Kallikak study proved to be a very potent indictment of the uneducated, of racial minorities, of the foreign-born, and of those classified as mentally retarded or mentally ill. The study, and others similar to it, was used by the privileged to justify the naturalness of their privileges—only the "good stock" was capable of acquiring and managing power and prerogatives. In addition to creating more and larger institutions for those persons deemed deficient or defective, politicians could argue on this basis against the expenditure of funds for education, health, and housing for the "Kallikaks" of the land. The Kallikak story was also used to argue for the necessity for compulsory sterilization laws. The most important of the eugenic sterilization campaigns was the focus of my book with Ray Nelson, *The Sterilization of Carrie Buck*, published in 1989.

In 1924 Carrie Buck was committed to the State Colony for Epileptics and Feebleminded near Lynchburg, Virginia. Shortly after her commitment, the 18-year-old Caucasian girl was chosen to be the first person sterilized under

Virginia's new law. She was to become, thereby, a test case for the constitutionality of state intervention into a person's reproductive practices.

The right of the state to perform the operation was first challenged and heard in the Circuit Court of Amherst County. The trial was initiated by the chief administrator of the State Colony. Carrie's guardian in the case and her attorney were also appointed by the Colony. No witnesses were called in court on her behalf. The only arguments in her favor (against her sterilization) were references to legal questions. These were brief and technical.

The Amherst Circuit Court decided in favor of the state and ordered that Carrie should be sterilized. The case was appealed first in Virginia and the Circuit Court's decision was upheld. Finally, the case was heard by the United States Supreme Court. The majority opinion of the court was that Virginia's compulsory sterilization law was constitutional. Thus, the precedent was established which gave state governments the right to become arbiters of the reproductive practices of citizens who were deemed to be defective in some way.

In delivering the majority opinion in the decision, Justice Oliver Wendell Holmes said:

> We have seen more than once that the public welfare may call upon the best citizens for their lives. It would be strange if it could not call upon those who already sap the strength of the State for these lesser sacrifices, often felt to be much by those concerned, in order to prevent our being swamped with incompetence. It is better for all the world, if instead of waiting to execute degenerate offspring for crime, or to let them starve for their imbecility, society can prevent those who are manifestly unfit from continuing their kind. The principle that sustains compulsory vaccination is broad enough to cover cutting the Fallopian tubes...

Carrie Buck's sterilization case achieved a place in legal history and in the history of the social sciences. It is still used as a case study in law schools. Students in the social sciences who study issues related to mental retardation and social policy are often presented with the story and its historical implications. The saga of social Darwinism in America simply cannot be told without reference to the sterilization decision by the Supreme Court in Carrie's case.

Some historians have noted the unfortunate consequences of the precedent established through Carrie's sterilization. The fact that the validity of compulsory sterilization was endorsed by the highest court in a country that prided itself on its commitment to individual freedom had a global impact. Carrie, as the subject of the case, became an historical figure of international fame. Carrie, the person, lived a life marked by what had been erroneously claimed of her and decided about her by people of power and influence. These people, however, had little understanding of her true character and abilities. She was paroled from the institution not long after the surgery was performed. Carrie was married twice, but lamented late in her life that she had been unable to have children. She spent most of her adult life helping others. She was a trusted caregiver to elderly people and one of her employers told me that Carrie could not have been mentally retarded. Her competence was obvious, she said, in the quality of care she gave to those who depended on her. "There was nothing wrong with that woman's mind," said the employer. Indeed, mental health professionals who observed her late in her life found no evidence of mental retardation. After Carrie died in a nursing home in 1983 she was buried near the grave of a child. Ironically, it is the grave of her illegitimate daughter. It was the birth of this daughter out of wedlock that was the real reason that Carrie was institutionalized in 1924 and ultimately became the pawn in the sterilization case. Her daughter, Vivian, was taken into foster care after Carrie was institutionalized. She died at the age of nine. She was an honor student in school!

Carrie's sterilization was performed with little public notice. Her surgery, however, was to have international consequences. The precedent it set would influence social policy around the world and would change the lives of tens of thousands of people. Within ten years more than 27,000 compulsory sterilizations had been performed in the United States. Also within that decade thirty state governments had passed sterilization laws, many of them based on Virginia's model. Following Carrie's sterilization more than 4,000 people were sterilized at the State Colony which is now known as the Central Virginia Training Center. The practice was continued there until 1972. A total of 8,000 people were involuntarily sterilized in Virginia during those years and nationally more than 60,000 people underwent the same procedure.

Ultimately, Carrie's sterilization and the overall American compulsory sterilization movement influenced the development of the race hygiene program in Nazi Germany. On July 14, 1933, the model sterilization act developed by the eugenics advocate Harry Laughlin, the same model used by Virginia, became law in Germany. The German law was implemented swiftly and broadly. By the end of the first year that the law was in effect, according to S. J. Holmes, over 56,000 people had been found to be defective by special hereditary health courts and had been sterilized. Hitler's actions were applauded by American eugenicists. Sterilization proponent Paul Popenoe felt that the Germans were following a policy that was consistent with the best thinking of eugenicists throughout the world. K. M. Ludmerer quotes an editorial statement from the *Eugenical News* that concluded, "It is difficult to see how the new German Sterilization Law could, as some have suggested, be deflected from its purely eugenical purpose, and made an 'instrument of tyranny' for the sterilization of non-Nordic races." It would be many years before most American eugenicists would comprehend the connection between their own work and the stark atrocities of the Nazi regime.

It has been estimated that between 1933 and 1945, two million people were deemed defective and sterilized in Germany. Perhaps it is because of the awfulness of the other atrocities committed during this period that so little attention has been focused on this reality. The dimensions of this infringement on the basic rights of so many human beings are, however, staggering when carefully considered. Recognizing that the legal and social sources of this practice were largely American is chilling. The writer Abby Mann was shaken by this recognition and included a scene in *Judgement at Nuremberg* which portrayed this terrible truth. In this scene the defense attorney for an accused Nazi war criminal cross examines a prosecution witness. The witness, Dr. Wieck, had in his testimony criticized the defendant and the Nazi regime for its involvement in measures of involuntary sterilization. The defense attorney, Rolfe, questions the witness about his portrayal of involuntary sterilization as a uniquely Nazi practice:

ROLFE

Dr. Wieck, you referred to 'novel National Socialist measures introduced, among them sexual sterilization.' Dr. Wieck, are you aware that this was not invented by National Socialism, but had been advanced for years before as a weapon in dealing with the mentally incompetent and the criminal?

DR. WIECK

Yes. I am aware of that.

ROLFE

Are you aware that it has advocates among leading citizens in many other countries?

DR. WIECK

I am not an expert on such laws.

ROLFE

(Crisply) Then permit me to read one to you.

(ROLFE signals the CLERK in the dock to bring him a book. The CLERK comes forward and hands it to him.)

ROLFE

This is a High Court opinion upholding such laws in existence in another country. 'We have seen more than once that the public welfare may call upon the best citizens for their lives. It would be strange, indeed, if it could not call upon those who already sapped the strength of the State, for these lesser sacrifices, in order to prevent our being swamped by incompetence. It is better for all the world, if, instead of waiting to execute degenerate offsprings for crime or to let them starve for their imbecility, society can prevent their propagation by medical means in the first place. Three generations of imbeciles are enough.' Do you recognize it now, Dr. Wieck?

DR. WIECK

(with emphatic distaste) No, Sir, I don't.

ROLFE

(smiles a little)Actually, there is no particular reason why you should, since the opinion upholds the sterilization law in the State of Virginia, in the United States, and was written and delivered by that great American jurist, Supreme Court Justice Oliver Wendell Holmes.

(ROLFE puts down the book. ROLFE hands the book to the CLERK and turns to DR. WIECK)

ROLFE

Now, Dr. Wieck. In view of what you have just learned, can you still say that
this was a 'novel National Socialist measure?'

I am certain that Abby Mann based this scene on actual testimony at the
war crimes trials before the Nuremberg Military Tribunals. I have long been
intrigued by this scene and have wondered about its source. I searched the
records of the trials and found what very well could have been its basis. The
Nuremberg material is voluminous and my search was far from exhaustive. I
suspect that there were other incidences of American eugenic policies and
practices being used as defense arguments for Nazi war criminals. The case of
Otto Hofmann, however, was even more disturbing for me than Mann's
dramatization. This was a real defense based upon some of the jarring realities
of American eugenics.

Otto Hofmann was a high ranking SS officer and was one of the facilitators
of policies aimed at what the Nazis conceptualized as the "final solution to the
Jewish question." He was head of what was called the Race and Settlement
Main Office of the Reichsfuehrer-SS. A copy of a memo to Hofmann from one
of his superiors dated April, 1942 was published after the war in a document
entitled *Nazi Conspiracy and Aggression*. It is filled with references to the final
solution and the problem of mixed marriages between Aryans and those of
"inferior" Jewish blood. A single paragraph from the memo makes clear the
kind of charge Hofmann and others had been given by the architects of the
final solution:

> Those half-Jews who are capable of propagation should be given the choice to
> submit to sterilization or to be evacuated in the same manner as Jews. In the
> case of sterilization, as well as in that of evacuation of the half-Jew, the
> German-blooded spouse will have to be given the opportunity to effect the
> dissolution of the marriage. I see no objection to the German spouse's obtain-
> ing the possibility of divorcing his sterilized or evacuated spouse in a simplified
> procedure without the limitations of Par. 53 of the Marriage Law.

The fifth volume of *Trials of the War Criminals Before the Nuremberg
Military Tribunals* contains the record of the conviction of Otto Hofmann. It
states that the evidence "establishes beyond any reasonable doubt Hofmann's
guilt and criminal responsibility for the following criminal activities pursued in
the furtherance of the Germanization program: the kidnapping of alien children; forcible abortions on Eastern workers; taking away infants of Eastern
workers; the illegal and unjust punishment of foreign nationals for sexual
intercourse with Germans; hampering the reproduction of enemy nationals;
the forced evacuation and resettlement of foreign populations; the forced
Germanization of enemy nationals; and the utilization of enemy nationals as
slave labor."

While the fifth volume of records of the Nuremberg Tribunals contains
the conviction of Otto Hofmann, the fourth volume includes documents which
were entered in his defense. Among them is an abstract prepared in 1937 by

the Information Service of the Racial-Political Office of the Reich Administration. It concerns what are called "Race Protection Laws of Other Countries" and appears to have been entered as evidence on Hofmann's behalf to show that the practices he engaged in during the war were based on precedents from other "civilized" nations. It contains a litany of sterilization policies from various countries including:

DENMARK

Denmark was one of the first nations in Europe to pass a law permitting sterilization...The vital interests of the community, as it says in the preamble, are to take precedence over the interests of the individual. The feeble-minded are sterilized.

FINLAND

The draft of the Finnish law on the sterilization of persons with a hereditary disease goes back to 1929. The motion for the bill, which likewise provides for compulsory sterilization in specific cases, was passed in Parliament by a vote of 144 to 14.

NORWAY

Norway also has a sterilization law. Efforts aim on the one hand at 'securing a fertile breed' and on the other hand at 'seeing that the nation is freed from parasites'. Persons are sterilized who suffer from mental diseases or from imperfectly developed mental faculties and are therefore not capable of caring for themselves and their offspring by their own labor.

SWEDEN

The Swedish Parliament has occupied itself with the question of sterilization since 1922 and in 1929 passed a law in this respect. The voluntariness which was expressed in this at first was annulled by an amendment in 1934. Compulsory sterilization therefore exists and is applied in cases of insanity.

Next in the litany comes the most detailed discussion. It begins with mention of early laws in the United States which either were not tested or which were not used, and continues with a quote from the decision in Carrie Buck's case. Although the facts and language are not exactly correct in their interpretation, the message that many of Hofmann's acts were consistent with established social policy in the United States is indisputably accurate.

UNITED STATES OF AMERICA

Since 1907 sterilization laws have been passed in 29 States of the United States of America. Those affected by the law were primarily criminals, feeble-minded, insane, epileptics, alcoholic and narcotic addicts, as well as prostitutes. Although almost all states try to carry out sterilization on a voluntary basis the courts have more than once ordered compulsory sterilizations. In a judgement of the Supreme Court of [1927]...it says, among other things: 'It is better for everybody if society, instead of waiting until it has to execute degenerate offspring or leave them to starve because of feeble-mindedness can prevent obviously inferior individuals from propagating their own kind. The principle justifying compulsory vaccination is broad enough to cover the severing of the Fallopian tubes.'

There is another statement in this document submitted in Hofmann's defense that should catch the attention of any American and be the stimulus for careful reflection about our own history. In defining the precedence for racially exclusive social policies and practices the abstract includes these comments:

> The United States, however, also provides an example for the racial legislation of the world in another respect. Although it is clearly established in the Declaration of Independence that everyone born in the United States is a citizen of the United States and so acquires all the rights which an American citizen can acquire, impassable lines are drawn between the individual races, especially in the southern states. Thus in certain states Japanese are excluded from the ownership of land or real estate and they are prevented from cultivating arable land.
>
> Marriages between colored persons and whites are forbidden in no less than 30 of the Federal States. Marriages contracted in spite of this ban are declared invalid.

This statement was followed by a list of seven state laws prohibiting marriages between people of different races. These prohibited marriage between white people and people from a number of different racially designated groups including "Negroes, Indians, Mulattoes, and Mongolians."

In her book, *White Trash: The Eugenic Family Studies*, Nicole Hahn Rafter quite accurately portrays the family degeneracy studies as having been focused primarily on lower class white families, on the "poor white trash" of early twentieth century America. Although there are references in many of these studies to race mixing having occurred in the families at one point or another, the emphasis was always on the degeneracy of the poor white strain itself. When Carrie Buck's case was first heard in the Amherst Circuit Court a report was submitted to the court by Harry Laughlin, the author of the model sterilization law that Virginia had adopted. He had analyzed information on Carrie and her family and he offered his report in support of her being sterilized. In commenting on her heritage, Laughlin said, "These people belong to the shiftless, ignorant and worthless class of anti-social whites of the South...[they are an] ignorant and moving class of people..." Henry Goddard in his book on the Kallikak family made the following comments about the kind of lower socio-economic class white people who were the subjects of his study: "If all of the slum districts of our cities were removed tomorrow and model tenements built in their places, we would still have slums in a week's time because we have these mentally defective people who can never be taught to live otherwise than as they have been living. Not until we take care of this class and see to it that their lives are guided by intelligent people, shall we remove these sores from our social life." And so it was it was largely on the basis of these "white trash stories" that institutions for people classified as having hereditary mental defects grew in number and in size. Of course black people and people of other races were also placed in some of these institutions. The real impetus for their proliferation, however, was the "white trash" facet of the eugenic scare.

On this basis also compulsory sterilization laws were enacted and enforced on those poor white people viewed as being carriers of "bad seeds."

Otto Hofmann's defense document should remind us, however, that eugenic arguments and genealogical studies were also used as a claimed scientific basis for race separation. They were also used to attribute validity to the measures used for the control of what were argued to be inferior races. The chapters that follow will focus on eugenics as an instrument of scientific and political racism.

Ultimately all of the eugenic family studies became justifications for some form of genocidal action. The genocide that resulted from them was sometimes social, sometimes psychological and sometimes the literal physical death of groups marked by them. Regardless of the particular form, however, eugenic arguments and eugenics in the guise of scientific research led to genocide. The remainder of this book is a further accounting of people and events that I have discovered in my own personal attempt to understand the interactions which occurred between eugenics and social policy in the earlier years of this century. The lessons I have learned through this journey have made me very sensitive to what is done in the name of science and it has led me to be cautious concerning what are argued to be social, legal and political necessities. I offer this book to you, the reader, for your consideration in this same spirit of sensitivity and caution.

References

Buck v. Bell, (1927), 274 U.S. 200, 47 S. Ct. 584.

Goddard, H. H., (1912), *The Kallikak Family: A Study in the Heredity of Feeble-Mindedness*, New York: The Macmillan Co.

Holmes, S. J., (1936), *Human Genetics and Its Social Import,* New York: McGraw-Hill.

Ludmerer, K. M., (1972), *Genetics and American Society,* Baltimore: Johns Hopkins University Press.

Laughlin, H. H., (1929), *The Legal Status of Eugenical Sterilization*, Chicago: Psychopathic Laboratory of the Muncipal Court of Chicago.

Mann, Abby, (1961), *Judgement at Nuremberg*, London: Cassell.

Office of the U.S. Chief of Counsel for Prosecution of Axis Criminality, (1947), *Nazi Conspiracy and Aggression*, Supplement A, Washington D.C.: U.S. Government Printing Office.

Rafter, N. H., (1988), *White Trash: The Eugenic Family Studies, 1877–1919*, Boston: Northeastern University Press.

Trials of War Criminals Before the Nuremberg Military Tribunals, Vol. 4, (1950), Washington D. C.: U.S. Government Printing Office.

Trials of War Criminals Before the Nuremberg Military Tribunals, Vol. 5, (1950), Washington D. C.: U.S. Government Printing Office.

CHAPTER TWO:

Earnest Cox, John Powell and the Anglo-Saxon Clubs of America

Arguments for the racial superiority of the white race have long rested on claimed scientific foundations. During the long years of American slavery that "peculiar institution" of one human being owning another had, of course, been justified by biblical injunctions. These injunctions typically lead to the revelation that slavery was a necessary vehicle through which to accomplish the "white man's burden" of protecting and "christianizing" the black heathen. The authority of science, however, had also been consistently invoked in support of the position that black people were inherently inferior to the white race. Stephen Jay Gould in his book *The Mismeasure of Man* provides stunning documentation of the development of scientific racism and illustrates how very often science has served as the handmaiden of political, social and racial agendas.

It is not surprising then that the new science of eugenics was embraced by many of those who advocated the strict segregation of racial groups and the placing of limitations on the rights of citizenship of black people in the United States. One such advocate was Major Earnest Sevier Cox.

Cox was among those zealots who employed eugenic principles in a campaign to combat what they perceived to be a menacing threat to the survival of the white race in America. They argued that intermarriage and illicit sexual relationships between the black and white races threatened to "mongrelize" the purity of the white race. They warned that such relationships between the races were in fact a form of "race suicide." Basing their alarming cries on fundamental eugenic tenets, they claimed that the inferiority of the black race (the "bad blood") would always taint the superior qualities of the white race (the "good blood"). Some, in fact, argued that the hybrid of the two races would be inferior to either of the "pure" strains even though one of the "pure" strains was clearly inferior to the other.

Earnest Sevier Cox wrote a book entitled *White America* which was published in 1923. In his book Cox argued that the single greatest threat to the culture of the United States was the danger of race mixing. He portrayed black people as being "insanely" desirous of marrying white people in order to break the color line between the races and produce "whiter" descendants. He also portrayed black people as posing an economic threat, particularly to the poor white people with whom they competed for low paying jobs. While he suggested ways that the immediate racial and economic threats that the presence of black people in the United States created could be managed, he felt that there was only one ultimate resolution to these problems. Earnest Cox argued that only by repatriation, only by returning the black people of America to the Africa of their ancestors could "White America" be saved. He further rationalized that a return to Africa would be a salvation of the hope of the black race as well. He felt that in Africa black people would find a less demanding environment in which they would prove to competent whereas in the complexity of the American culture they were doomed to a future of incompetence.

> Repatriation will settle our Negro problem forever and will give the Negro a future... (p. 342).

Cox believed passionately, then, in the dual necessities of separation of the races as a temporary measure and repatriation as the ultimate answer to the race question in America. He continued to espouse these policies even in his very old age. When he was in his eighties he wrote the following statements which were published in 1972 in his book *Lincoln's Negro Policy*.

> Up until fairly recently the Negro was considered to be mostly a southern problem, and it was thought that throughout the rest of the nation that we must endure it as best we could. At least this general conviction allowed the Southern people a chance to work out their own race problems. Americans North, East and West also know that in spite of all of our many difficulties including the terrible days of Reconstruction and the present oppression of the South by the Federal Government, that our color line is drawn and remains virtually intact. Notwithstanding the civil rights laws, presidential executive degrees and court decisions this line separates those who are white and those not white, and they know that in its practical application it is the most effective color line in existence. They know that though our color line has not prevented mixbreeds it has kept the mixbreeds on the Negro side of the color line, and in so doing has preserved an unquestioned white population of many millions.
>
> For this great contribution to America the people of the nation owe an incalculable debt to the White South they will never be able to repay. Is it then asking too much that the whole nation now acknowledge this great service by wholeheartedly supporting a separation of the races by a resettlement of American Negroes in Africa? By doing this it would honor our heritage as a white people and at the same time honor the heritage of the Negro people.
>
> The white and Negro people of America must abandon their support of the mulatto integrationists and assist the self respecting Negro nationalists in a crusade to provide for the voluntary repatriation of American Negroes in Africa...all that we need is will, and once this is understood and applied to the Negro problem it will be solved in the only way it can be solved, and that is by separation of the races (pp. 144–145).

Illustration 1: Earnest S. Cox circa 1972. From *Lincoln's Negro Policy* by Earnest S. Cox.

In *Lincoln's Negro Policy* Cox explains that he had traveled and studied extensively in Africa, Asia and South America, and that after serving in the military in World War I, he moved from his native Tennessee and settled in Richmond, Virginia. While earning his living as a real estate agent, he devoted his efforts otherwise to writing about his perceptions of the race issue. Eventually he became acquainted with people in influential social circles in Richmond and shared his writings with some of them. He described how he met one Richmond man who was to become a powerful ally:

> ...through Mrs. Ragland, I met Miss Margaret Rackett, secretary to Mr. Archer Jones, the founder of the Duplex Envelope Company and the leading promoter of the renewed interest in [Edgar Allen] Poe. Miss Rackett talked to Mr. Jones about my manuscript, *White America*. He read the manuscript and invited me to his home for dinner. He told me that John Powell, the distinguished musician, was a man of gifted intellect and that he would be interested in the manuscript.
>
> My meeting with Powell was to lead to a close and sustained friendship...Powell, who had been educated at the University of Virginia and in Europe, quickly showed an interest in my manuscript, *White America*. When returning from Europe, where he had not seen the Negro and the white in racial contact, he was impressed [negatively] by the racial intermingling in the United States and had written on our race problem. The substance of his manuscript covered a portion of that of mine (pp. 16–17).

Indeed John Powell was a distinguished and powerful person in the social and political structures of Virginia of that time. He would also prove to be forceful and effective in implementing the racial ideals that he and Cox shared.

John Powell was born in Richmond in 1882. Both of his parents were from families of longstanding prominence. From early in his life he must have been immersed in a sense of his own aristocracy and the traditional values of his family. Certainly my reading of correspondence in his collected papers at the University of Virginia gave me the impression that he thought of himself and interacted with others as a "Virginia Gentleman" in an almost stereotypical way. After graduating from the University of Virginia in 1901, Powell studied piano and music composition in Europe for several years. He performed concerts both abroad and in the United States, and soon won international recognition as a performer and composer.

It is interesting to note that the artistic achievement which initially brought him world recognition was his composition for piano and orchestra entitled *Rhapsodie Negre*. It is ironic that, given his opinions and later activities, he achieved fame through a piece consisting of nostalgic themes of black life. Powell performed *Rhapsodie Negre* in almost every major city in the United States and Europe.

It is also ironic that John Powell would later deny the importance of black music to the musical heritage of America. In an article entitled "How America Can Develop a National Music" which appeared in the journal *The Etude* in

1927, Powell commenting on the contributions of black culture to American music said:

> Formerly I, myself, made certain contributions to this field in my 'Sonata Virginianesque'...and more recently in my 'Rhapsodie Negre' for piano and orchestra. In my own case, however, the expression was purely objective and was frankly intended to be character music. I do not consider that this school has much value to contribute to a national American music. When the negro music is analyzed, we see at once that that part of it which is purely negro is almost as meager and monotonous as the Indian music [in an earlier section of the article Powell had also discounted the influence of Native Americans on American music.] Many of the best known negro songs are now known to be not folk-songs at all, but the compositions of white men, as, for example, the Stephen Foster songs. And the negro spirituals, it has now been discovered, are also chiefly European in their origin, being merely negro adaptations of white campmeeting and revival tunes of the last century. Most of these spirituals, when critically analyzed, show clearly in their melodic and harmonic structure their Caucasian origin (p. 349).

Powell went on in the article to dismiss all influences on American music except those from Anglo-Saxon cultural traditions. Here, he believed, lay the origins and the strengths of American music. His adoration of things Anglo-Saxon, however, was far from being limited to music.

By 1923 John Powell had begun to express his racial sentiments in professional writings and in lectures which were ostensibly focused on American music. In "Music and the Nation," published by Rice University, he commented on black-white miscegenation and predicted that in the United States this "contamination" of the races would lead to eventual degeneration of the whole Caucasian race and thereby to the annihilation of white civilization. He also spoke strongly in support of deporting the black people of America back to Africa. In the same context Powell called for stricter immigration laws for non-Anglo-Saxon immigrants. He felt that existing laws allowed entrance for too much inferior stock from less desirable parts of the world. The influence of eugenic thought is evident in these remarks.

In the fall of 1922 Powell, along with Earnest Sevier Cox, founded the Anglo-Saxon Clubs of America. An article in the *Richmond News Leader* the following June described the goals of the organization:

> The fundamental purpose of the organization is the preservation and maintenance of Anglo-Saxon ideals and civilization in America. This purpose is to be accomplished in three ways: first, by the strengthening of Anglo-Saxon instincts, traditions and principles among representatives of our original American stock; second, by intelligent selection and exclusion of immigrants; and third, by fundamental and final solutions of our racial problems in general, most especially of the Negro problem (p. 5).

Also included in the *News Leader* article was a petition. Under Powell's leadership the Anglo-Saxon Clubs [by then there were several chapters] were seeking signatures endorsing the following motions:

Illustration 2: John Powell circa 1937. Photograph courtesy of Special Collections, Alderman Library, University of Virginia.

1. There shall be instituted immediately a system of registration and birth certificates showing the racial composition (white, black, brown, yellow, red) of every resident of this state.

2. No marriage license shall be granted save upon presentation and attestation under oath by both parties of said registration or birth certificate.

3. White persons may only marry whites.

4. For the purposes of this legislation, the term 'white persons' shall apply only to individuals who have no trace whatsoever of any blood other than Caucasian (p. 5).

The petition was to be presented to the General Assembly of Virginia at its next session.

On February 13, 1924 a front page article in the *Richmond Times-Dispatch* carried the headline, "Powell Asks Law Guarding Racial Purity." His presentation to the legislature was described as a "powerful appeal" from the President of the Anglo-Saxon Clubs of America. The *Times-Dispatch* became a vigorous supporter of Powell's cause and published an editorial a few days later that must have added momentum to the race integrity legislative effort. Entitled "Racial Integrity" it appeared on February 18, the day the bill was to be considered, and included the following observations:

...In no other part of the world is there a race problem of such magnitude as the one we face today. It is a matter that gives thinking men very serious food for thought. Unfortunately the solution of it has not yet commended itself to the less thoughtful persons as a vital necessity. That is because they have not pondered what it means to have two distinct races, the one vastly inferior to the other, living together on terms of political equality and having every opportunity for the co-mingling of blood.

Unless stringent measures are adopted to keep the races separate in the matter of marriage, amalgamation is inevitable. It will, perhaps, be a long process, but it will be consummated. One race will absorb the other. And history shows the more highly developed strain always is the one to go. America is headed toward mongrelism, only a realization of the seriousness of that fact, and resultant measures to retain racial integrity can save the country from becoming negroid in population. Every recognized ethnologist is as certain of that as he is that the sun rose this morning.

In Virginia, the intermingling of the races is all too apparent. There are hundred of instances in which it has become impossible, without a diligent search into the records or an exhaustive investigation among community elders, to establish racial contamination. Thousands of men and women who pass for white persons in this state have in their veins Negro blood. If they are allowed to intermarry with pure Caucasians, and they are doing it now, the way is being paved for a complete breakdown of the races. Negro blood in time will predominate. That is a truth no scientist or student of history will doubt for a moment.

...There is in the bill nothing to give offense to the right-thinking colored man. He, as well as his white friend, is anxious to preserve his racial integrity. The co-mingling of blood does not help the negro—no admixture of strains, even in the lower animal world, ever results in progeny with as many good qualities as adhere to either of the originals—and it will sound the death knell of the white man. Once a drop of inferior blood gets in his veins, he descends lower and lower in the mongrel scale.

The bill which the Senate considers today is a test of the Caucasian's willingness to take such steps as will preserve his strain in all its purity. It means a great deal to the race, and to Virginia is given the opportunity to lead the way for her sister States. If this measure is passed, it may presage a national movement on behalf of racial integrity (p. 6).

The editorial may have helped the cause. John Powell's appeal, the petition he presented to the legislature, other newspaper support, and perhaps other political forces resulted in the passage of the legislation. The "Race Integrity Law" became effective in Virginia on June 15, 1924.

With the publicity given to the consideration and passage of the law, John Powell's image as a leader and spokesman for the movement grew. My review of his papers at the University of Virginia revealed that during this period he received many requests to make public presentations and that his opinions on racial issues were highly regarded by many powerful individuals and influential groups. Indeed, by 1926 he was afforded the opportunity to present his views and those of the Anglo-Saxon Clubs in a series of eleven parts entitled "The Last Stand" which was published in the *Times-Dispatch* during February and March. Powell obviously used the series to reach the general public but he was also very likely employing it as a vehicle for lobbying the General Assembly. In 1926 he was involved in urging the legislature to correct what he and his colleagues considered to be problems with the 1924 law. Several modifications were proposed. First, the 1924 bill had categorized persons with more than one-sixteenth "Indian blood" as non-white. The proposed modification would have tightened the definition of "white" and would have forbidden the marriage of a white person to anyone with *any* "known, demonstrable, or ascertainable admixture" of Indian blood. This was *very upsetting* to some of the prominent Virginia families who had long and proudly claimed descent from John Rolfe and Pocahontas and a few other socially acceptable Native American lines. Apparently they took severe exception to being classified or having their ancestors labeled as being non-white when they had for so long thought of themselves as being pure, prestigious and, in some cases, among the First Families of Virginia (the FFVs). This provision was not, to say the least, included in the bill that passed in the legislature. It is interesting to note that one of Powell's biographers was Pocahontas Wright Edmunds who was a lineal descendent in two lines from Pocahontas. In her 1972 book, *Virginians Out Front*, she speaks of having known Powell well and having entertained he and his wife as houseguests on two occasions. She describes him in very heroic terms:

> The man who had dominated Virginia's music for sixty years, a musician more honored than any musician had been in any other state, he was that exception to the rule, a prophet in his own country. His prophecy was that American music must find itself in its Anglo-American folk roots. His compo-

sitions, his playing of them, and his eager life, alert to the end, had shown how (pp. 373–374).

A second element of the 1926 bill was that it made "carnal communication" between whites and non-whites a felony. This measure, of course, was meant to curb race mixing outside the bonds of marriage. Curiously enough, this provision was also not included in the act that was approved by the General Assembly. A third part of the bill called for enforced separation of the races in places of entertainment. This was the only provision of the bill which passed in the General Assembly in March.

John Powell's musical career and his political activities might appear to some people to be separate and distinct spheres of his life. He did not view them as such, however, and some music scholars have interpreted his compositions as being very expressive of his social and racial philosophy. L. Moody Simms in an article entitled "Folk Music in America: John Powell and the 'National Musical Idiom'" commented on Powell's *Rhapsodie Negre*.

> In the *Negre Rhapsody*, Powell utilized Negro spirituals, dance rhythms, and street tunes...The work begins with a mighty sigh, a primal wail, and a savage dance, followed by a calmer moment when the theme of *Swing, Low, Sweet Chariot* is introduced. However, the idealization which creeps in during the middle section cannot maintain itself against the primitive instinct. This part of the work builds to a climax which collapses with a crash. The remainder of the piece is orgiastic and pagan, ending on a note of despair and ultimate tragedy (p. 511).

In his book, *Our American Music: Three Hundred Years Of It*, John Tasker Howard quotes Donald Francis Tovey, the Edinburgh music critic, as saying:

> Mr. Powell has the profoundest respect for the Negro as artist and human being. But profound sympathy is very different from the facile sentimentality that refuses to recognize the dangers that threaten two races of widely different stages of evolution that try to live together. The *Rhapsodie Negre* is music, not political propaganda; but it will be soonest understood by those who, whether from personal knowledge of the composer or from the capacity to recognize emotional values in music, manage to understand from the outset that this is not only an eminently romantic, but also a thoroughly tragic piece (p. 457).

Howard closes his commentary on Powell by describing him as being a significant artist for a number of reasons. He characterizes his music as primal, salty and vital. Howard, as Powell's contemporary, saw him as:

> ...such an intense person himself, that his almost feverish temperament creeps into all that he writes—yet with some exquisitely lyric moments in between. And lastly, and possibly most important, his social and political creed makes him a nationalist, typical of the Anglo-Saxon southern aristocracy, with fixed racial ideas that are thoroughly apparent in his music. He is a prophet of the white South (p. 459).

References

"Anglo-Saxon Club...," (1923), *Richmond News Leaders*, June 5, p. 5.

Cox, Earnest S., (1923), *White America*, Richmond, VA: White America Society.

_____, (1972), *Lincoln's Negro Policy*, Richmond, VA: Earnest S. Cox.

Edmunds, Pocahontas, (1972), *Virginians Out Front*, Richmond, VA: Whittlet and Shepperson.

Howard, John T., (1939), *Our American Music: Three Hundred Years of It*, New York: Thomas Y. Crowell.

Powell, John, (1923), "Music and the nation." *The Rice University Pamphlet*, X, No. 3, pp. 127–163.

"Powell Asks Law...," (1924), *Richmond Times-Dispatch*, February 13, pp. 1–2.

Powell, John, (1927), "How America can develop a national music," *The Etude*, May.

"Racial Integrity," (1924), *Richmond Times-Dispatch*, February 18, p. 6.

Simms, L. Moody, (1973), "Folk music in America: John Powell and the 'National Musical Idiom'." *Journal of Popular Culture*, Vol. 7, No. 3, pp. 51–515.

"The Last Stand," (1926), *Richmond Times-Dispatch*, February 15 – March 2.

CHAPTER THREE:

John Powell and Marcus Garvey — The Peculiar Alliance

The concept of repatriation to Africa of black people from the United States did not, of course, originate with Earnest Cox and John Powell. They were revisiting an idea that had been advocated for many years. Abraham Lincoln proposed a voluntary African colonization program for the slaves he had emancipated. This was the source of Earnest Cox's choice of the title *Lincoln's Negro Policy* for one of his books. Lincoln was unsuccessful in securing an appropriation from Congress to support such a program. Following this failure little attention was given for a while to repatriation. The first two decades of the twentieth century, however, were to yield not only the repatriation proposals of Powell and Cox, but others. A call for the return to Africa for the black people of the United States was to come from a brilliant and charismatic black leader. His name was Marcus Garvey.

Garvey was Jamaican by birth and is considered a national hero there today. When he founded the Universal Negro Improvement Association (U.N.I.A.) in Jamaica in 1914 his ideas were not, however, well received there. Seeking a more fertile environment for his proposals for race separation, rugged black individualism and repatriation, he came to the United States. Here his ideas were embraced in several quarters. Edmond Cronon analyzes the appeal of Garvey's philosophy and the goals of the U.N.I.A. in his 1969 book entitled *The Story of Marcus Garvey and the Universal Negro Improvement Association*. According to Cronon, Garvey's philosophy moved the focus of thought away from how equality could be achieved within predominantly white cultures. He did not believe that white Americans would ever be converted to the idea of sharing political, social, and economic resources equitably with black people and he argued, therefore, that struggling for equality in the United States was futile. Instead, he professed, black people should concentrate on establishing their own nation in Africa. Garvey's advocacy of the abandonment of the struggle for equality and his emphasis on an African migration won him the open support of the premier racist organization in the United States, the Ku Klux Klan. His work was also approved of and supported by John Powell's Anglo-Saxon Clubs of America. A revealing measure, perhaps, of good feelings between the Anglo-Saxon Clubs and the

U.N.I.A. is one pointed out by Cronon. Marcus Garvey's book, *Philosophy and Opinions*, a volume directed to black people, carried an advertisement for Earnest Cox's polemic on race separation and race purity, *White America* (p. 188).

In October of 1923 Marcus Garvey wrote "An Appeal to the Soul of White America." Excerpts from that appeal may help to illustrate Garvey's philosophy and its attractiveness to men like John Powell and Earnest Cox.

> In another one hundred years white America will have doubled its population; in another two hundred years it will have trebled itself. The keen student must realize that the centuries ahead will bring us an over-crowded country; opportunities, as the population grows larger, will be fewer; the competition for bread between the people of their own class will become keener, and so much more so will there be no room for two competitive races, the one strong, and the other weak... (p. 4).

Garvey spoke of a coming generation of educated and ambitious black men and women, a generation who would be capable of filling the highest and most prized positions in the society, in industry, commerce, government and politics. He asked if they could possibly be held back. If they were, he predicted, this new generation of black people would agitate and throw the constitution in the faces of the white power structure.

> Can you stand before civilization and deny the truth of your constitution? What are you going to do then? You who are just will open the door of opportunity and say to all and sundry, 'Enter in.' But, ladies and gentlemen, what about the mob, that starving crowd of your own race? Will they stand by, suffer and starve, and allow an opposite, competitive race to prosper in the midst of their distress? If you can conjure these things up in your mind, then you have the vision of the race problem of the future in America (p. 4).

Garvey felt that there was only one possible solution. That solution was to provide a separate outlet for the energies, ambitions, and passions of America's black people. The answer was to surround the race with opportunities of its own.

> The Negro must have a country and a nation of his own...We have found a place; it is Africa, and as black men for three centuries have helped white men build America, surely generous and grateful white men will help black men build Africa (pp. 4–5).

By the time Garvey wrote this appeal he had encountered serious legal problems. He had formed a fleet of three ships as part of his plan to transport black people "back" to Africa. He created a company called the Black Star Shipping Line and sold stock to finance the enterprise. The company failed financially and Garvey was indicted on charges of mail fraud. This indictment rested on claims that he had continued to sell stock in the Black Star Line through the mail even though he was aware that the company was insolvent. He was convicted of the fraud charge and was imprisoned at the Atlanta Federal Penitentiary in early 1925.

Marcus Garvey's trial and imprisonment seems to have intensified the support he received from race separatists and white supremacists. I must admit that in the process of doing research for this book I was on several occasions simply amazed to come across documents which portrayed a spirit of admiration and cooperation between the Universal Negro Improvement Association and the Anglo-Saxon Clubs of America. Given that experience it is easy for me to imagine that in 1925 many people would have had difficulty in understanding such a relationship or accepting its credulity.

In the John Powell Collection there is a handwritten draft of a letter which Powell sent to the editor of *The Negro World*, the newspaper published by the Universal Negro Improvement Association, on August 22, 1925. Portions of that letter depict Powell's views of his relationship to Garvey and the U.N.I.A.

The Anglo-Saxon Clubs of America is a non-secret, non-fraternal and non-sectarian organization...Its general purpose is the preservation of Anglo-Saxon civilization and ideals in America—the civilization and ideals of the founders of our Country. This purpose it seeks to attain by working for the preservation of racial integrity. The Racial Integrity law which it proposed and which the General Assembly of Virginia enacted at its last session, brought no hardship nor insult to the negro race...In spirit and in effect the law is in absolute accord with the principles of the U.N.I.A. and of Marcus Garvey, as announced in his 'Appeal to the Soul of White America.' The ideal of racial integrity must appeal as strongly to self-respecting negroes as to self-respecting whites, since amalgamation would bring about equally the death of both races as ethnological entities.

...The charge that Marcus Garvey has formed an alliance with the Anglo-Saxon Clubs is being circulated by his enemies, in order to discredit him with his own people and race, and to weaken his influence with the U.N.I.A. There would be nothing discreditable to Garvey if such an alliance had been formed; as a matter of fact, there is no alliance, nor has an alliance been discussed or ever considered. The only basis of this falsehood is that I visited Garvey when in Atlanta last June; the purpose of my visit was to take him a friendly message from Major E. S. Cox, and to express to him my admiration for his courageous leadership and indignation at the persecution he was forced to endure. I was amazed at his patience under affliction, his freedom from rancor, his wisdom and his enthusiasm in the cause of his people. In the course of our conversation, I told him that in his 'Appeal to the Soul of White America' he had profoundly touched and moved at least one American. In return, he assured me that he and the U.N.I.A. were unalterably opposed to racial amalgamation.

On my return to Richmond, I reported this conversation to the Richmond Post of the Anglo-Saxon Clubs of America. My talk on this occasion was correctly published in the *Richmond Times-Dispatch* and so came to the notice of the *Norfolk Journal and Guide* [a black publication], which in its next issue magnified and distorted the whole affair, thus starting the attack on Garvey in the Negro press.

At the last meeting of the Richmond Post of A.S.C.O.A., by unanimous vote, an expression of sympathy and encouragement was sent to the President

Illustration 3: Marcus Garvey. From *Philosophy and Opinions of Marcus Garvey,* by Amy Jacques-Garvey. Published by The Universal Publishing House in New York in 1923.

of the Richmond Chapter of the U.N.I.A., and two nights later a delegation from the Anglo-Saxon Post attended the meeting of the U.N.I.A. in order to demonstrate to Amy Jacques Garvey, the principal speaker of the evening, their approval and sympathy for herself and her husband in their efforts for the integrity and independence of the negro race. The white visitors were treated with every courtesy, and heard with enthusiastic approval the notable speeches of the occasion.

This apparent and contrived friendship between black and white separatists continued to grow. Less than a week after Powell wrote his letter to the *Negro World*, Marcus Garvey drafted a letter to the Harlem chapter of the Universal Negro Improvement Association introducing John Powell. Powell was scheduled to speak to the organization and Garvey wanted him accepted by the organization as a friend. He spoke of his friendship with Powell as "sturdy, honorable and sincere." He also spoke in glowing terms of the Anglo-Saxon Clubs of America. Again, it seems curious to hear the man who by this time had become known as "Black Moses" by his followers speaking so positively of an organization that held firmly to the tenet of the basic inferiority of the black race.

> Mr. Powell represents a body of men and women for whom I maintain the greatest respect because of their honesty and lack of hypocrisy. They represent the clean-cut and honest section of the white race that uncompromisingly stands for the purity of their race, even as we unhesitatingly and determinedly agitate and fight for the purity of the Negro race. All races should be pure in morals and in outlook, and for that we, as Negroes, admire the leaders and members of the Anglo-Saxon Clubs. They are honest and honorable in their desire to purify and preserve the white race even as we are determined to purify and standardize our race (p. 338).

Garvey went on to say that the two organizations should work together. He saw their common purposes as being race purity, race separation, and freedom of self-development and self-expression. By this time both organizations had spoken disparagingly of the N.A.A.C.P. which was at that time and remained for decades the major organization pushing for racial equality, a term that was anathema to both Garvey and Powell. It was most likely the N.A.A.C.P. Garvey was referring to when he made the following statement in his introduction:

> Those who are against this [race purity and separation] are enemies of both races, and rebels against morality, nature and God; for acting to the contrary, no good or ethical purpose can be served, but a continuation of world confusion, immorality and sin (pp. 338–339).

When Powell spoke to the Harlem chapter of the U.N.I.A. he referred with gratitude to the positive reception that Earnest Cox's *White America* had been given by members of the organization. He quoted one leader of that group as saying that the book should be in every black person's home "along with the Bible." He also congratulated the membership for seeing the race situation in America clearly and having the courage to face the facts of the situation. He presented himself as not merely a white American but also as a

Virginian, a Southerner, and as the descendent of slave owners. In this regard he portrayed himself as the representative of a South that did not harbor racial hatred but was motivated by a desire to do what was genuinely best for both races.

Powell argued that there was no truly free black person in the United States. He explained:

> The war did not make you free, and constitutional amendments did not make you free and the N.A.A.C.P. has not made you free...Why is it that you are not free? What I am going to say to you is nothing new to you.
> You are not free because the civilization that you are living under is not your own (p. 346).

Powell concluded his speech with a tribute to Marcus Garvey. He implied that Garvey had been convicted and imprisoned for political reasons and that black and white factions alike had conspired to have him removed from the public arena;

> ...if the white people in the South of this country realized that Marcus Garvey was standing not only for the salvation of his own race but for the salvation of the white race as well—if they realized that he had been railroaded into prison merely because he did not have a white face—if they realized what he stood for and what he meant, I believe that the South would rise to a man and demand that your great leader be released and restored to you...Your enemies in your own race have the help and support of white people; white people give them money; white people go and flatter them and hold out false hopes to them and hob-nob with them, and offer them social equality and put up money to help them; and some of those white people are of great wealth and influence. I want to tell you this: that man for man we can match them...
> I noticed when I came in, the first things that struck my eye were some tags which all of you are wearing, and I looked at them and I saw 'Let him go.' I want to offer an amendment—free him; we don't want to let him go; we want to keep him here to do this work... And, my friends, if there is any honor in the American nation, I can promise you that when Marcus Garvey is free he shall not be deported [to Jamaica] (p. 349).

The degree to which John Powell's dedication to Marcus Garvey's philosophy and movement was opportunistic and manipulative is a question that is not easily resolved. After studying his papers in this regard, however, I have reached the conclusion that there was a marked and significant gulf between his public statements of support for the U.N.I.A. and his private (and at times not so private) actions. The reasons for his public support for Garvey's movement are perhaps best portrayed through a letter he wrote in September of 1925 to Thomas Dabney, a black student who was preparing a paper on Garvey's work. Dabney had written to Powell earlier in the year requesting information and had emphasized in his letter that "I am a Virginian not a Northern meddler as you might think. I am very much interested in the race problem and such bills as are being proposed for its solution." In response Powell sent Dabney a long and detailed explanation of his support for Garvey.

Portions of that letter are quoted here as clear indicators of Powell's public rationale for his support of Garvey:

> Politically, the Garvey movement must be considered from two points of view: first, as affecting the internal politics of America; second, as affecting international or world politics. In connection with the first viewpoint, the most obvious and striking thought is this: the withdrawal, on the part of a large body of Negroes, of their demand for social and political equality, —their definite acceptance of the status of temporary sojourners in a land not their home land, in which, despite legal and constitutional guarantees, they suffer many of the disabilities of aliens, must inevitably lead to radical changes in the political and sectional alignment of parties. It will tend largely to remove the Negro problem from the cockpit of party politics where it has been unscrupulously used in equal degree as capital by both national parties...
>
> From the international point of view, it is obvious that a great movement, inspired by a flaming sense of nationality and race consciousness, and, in many respects, analogous to Jewish Zionism, must produce, in the field of world politics, even more far-reaching and profound consequences than has the Zionist movement. As Mesopotamia was the real bone of contention in the recent World War, so Africa, the richest undeveloped territory in the world, bids fair to become the cause of the next conflict of nations. The European Powers, uneasy with their sense of guilt on account of their cruelty and rapacity, must view with grave alarm the prospect of any considerable influx of American Negroes into the Dark Continent. They dread the effect on the natives of the influence of these American Negroes, educated, trained under American ideas of efficiency, ablaze with the fervor of racial aspiration. But whether the great powers wish it or no, Africa is for the Africans...
>
> I am convinced that geographical separation is the only possible means of preserving racial integrity. Whether such separation could be maintained permanently or no, is not the problem of the present but of the future. Certain it is, that racial contact, as always in the past, inevitably leads to eventual amalgamation. If the Negro remains in America, both races will disappear as ethnological entities and will be supplanted by a race of hybrids. This would mean the end of white civilization in America, and the death of all hopes of the development of a typical African culture among the descendants of the American Negroes. It is not necessary, in reaching this conclusion, to postulate negro inferiority. Just as in chemistry, two harmless, or even beneficent, substances, when mixed, may form a deadly poison, so, in biology, two varieties, each of excellent qualities, may be interbred with disastrous results, irrespective of relative superiority or inferiority...Interbreeding between the African and the Caucasian has invariably, in the past, resulted in cultural decay. Such an eventuality in America would be disastrous to both races (pp. 1–3).

In the next chapter I think it will become clear that John Powell's ideas and actions did not in fact follow his confessed support of Marcus Garvey's movement to promote pride in the black race. As an important illustration of his lack of responsiveness to the substance of the movement, however, it is worthwhile to consider a letter sent to Powell on March 26, 1926. The letter

Illustration 4: John Powell as a young man. Photograph courtesy of Special Collections, Alderman Library, University of Virginia.

came from the President of a small black college at Claremont near Jamestown, Virginia. The Temperance Industrial and Collegiate Institute had been founded in 1892 by Dr. John Smallwood. Smallwood was, interestingly enough, a grandson of Nat Turner, the leader of the slave revolt in 1831 which became symbolic of the nation's ordeal of facing the issue of slavery. Smallwood was thoroughly committed to the college and struggled to keep it viable until his early death at age 49 in 1912. The man writing Powell was a successor to Smallwood named Caleb Robinson. On the envelope Mr. Robinson had written and underlined "Strictly personal—If not here please forward and oblige." He pleaded for confidentiality in the letter as well and then proceeded to explain to Powell his reason for writing. As with other original correspondence and documents quoted in this book, the spelling and punctuation have been left as I found them in the letter.

With this introduction, I shall now tell you something that is deep down in my heart, and which I ask that you keep a profound secret. I am a true and tried member of the Universal Negro Improvement Association with headquarters in New York City and an ardent admirer, believer and supporter of the great Negro leader and martyr, the Hon. Marcus Garvey. I am a true disciple of his 'Back to Africa' and 'Africa for the Africans' movements. I am searching in Virginia and in the South for friends of Marcus Garvey and 'Garveyism' especially among your people in this most critical moment in the history and future of the Negro race.

The benevolent institution of learning at Claremont, Va. of which I am president, has a wonderful history. It was established thirty (35) five years ago, by a black man named Jno J. Smallwood, whose home was in Richmond where he died from overwork in the interest of the training of his people... Here is something noteworthy and remarkable. This school occupies the spot where the second cargo of Negro slaves landed in 1622 and is in sight of Jamestown, the old English settlement where the first cargo landed in 1619. The school owns the very wharf with 65 acres of land on the historical 'James.' The place is unique, running with the river about two miles, on a respectable elevation where great and lofty trees, heavy with age, stand and look down upon the waters running to join the ocean, like sentinels guarding some eternal destiny, and with mute significance tell a story thrilling and wonderful.

This black man, Smallwood, was born a slave child on the very spot. Three days after his birth his mother was sold from him, and he was left to God. He grew up, received an education, South and North, went back to Claremont, and with the help of his friends, especially white, bought the slave pen where he was born, and the wharf where his ancestors landed as slaves, and sixty (65) five acres of land surrounding them, and established there what was known as 'Temperance Industrial and Collegiate Institute,' a strictly Christian school for the training and discipline of the descendants of those same slaves who landed there, bled there, died there and were sold there over 300 years ago. The Hon. Jno Hay, once Sec'y of State of the United States of America, was his friend and helped him largely to erect the building known as 'Lincoln Hall'... Besides this building there are about eight (8) others of smaller size and an electric power plant capable of heating and lighting a good size town... The location is beautiful almost beyond comparison and adjoins the old historical Allen Mansion, where Edgar Allen Poe lived and is said to have written the 'Raven' and many others of his noted poems.

Now, I am telling you these things to say that because of the history of the place, and its sacredness to our group, we are deciding to make it the Southern Headquarters of the Garvey 'Back to Africa' movement, and have there a greater school to teach and train boys and girls, men and women of African descent in the 'Back to Africa Movement' and the possibilities of 'Africa for Africans'—to so train them here that when they depart to live in Africa they will on arriving be an asset and not a liability there, for as you well understand it is going to take some time before we can remove the American Negro as a whole to their fatherland, and what we now do must be done carefully, quickly and well—satisfactory to the masses.

We want the Universal Negro Improvement Association to own, and possess and occupy this place and those who know about this movement, are enthusiastic over the idea. But I am pained to say that there is a debt of about $60,000/Sixty Thousand Dollars on the property. [The holders of the mortgage] have served notice on us that except we settle with them by the 9th of April, they will advertise the property for sale to the highest bidder. We have not the money, and at present the Garvey people have not the money to meet these payments and take the property over. They are elated over the idea of getting possession of this most valuable place as a 'Southern Educational Headquarters' and from these very waters and that very wharf where Negroes from Africa landed and were slaves from over 300 years send the sons and daughters of those very slaves trained at the very spot—embarking from the very wharf on ships to Africa their fatherland, to help regain it and make it forever 'Africa for Africans.' Is not this a wonderful inspiration and does it not seem a very 'Godsend.' Does it not appear remarkable and the linking up of historical events right in Virginia, the Mother of States and the Old Dominion?...Now—please hear this: The trustees under whom I work are all Colored men of Virginia but one. They do not have the money to meet the obligations, and I can't raise it anywhere by April the 9th. They have almost decided to turn the property over to the American Baptist Home Mission Society with headquarters at New York and get out of it. This is a white organization that supports schools for negroes in the South, having a school at Richmond known as Virginia Union University. In this case the property and School at Claremont will pass entirely from the ownership of our group forever, and our dear and cherished scheme will be killed altogether. The very thought makes my heart bleed.

I, with one or two others of the trustees are the only ones holding out against turning the property over to a white association...We cannot hold out successfully except we get speedy help from some source—before the 9th April. The Phila. Division of the U.N.I.A. is working on the proposition until the parent body can take hold but they will not be able to raise the money by the 9th of April as the 5th International Convention of the U.N.I.A. is now in session at Detroit, Mich. where I went as a delegate, and am now on my way home with grief in my heart [the letter was postmarked Pittsburgh]. Let me further say that the Sec'y and over half of the trustees of the School live in Richmond, and are prominent Colored men; but they are *not interested* in the Garvey movement, for reasons that you understand or may imagine and which I shall not mention here. I, with the few who are deeply interested, are in the minority and are outvoted on this issue. We are, therefore, keeping the matter of turning the property over to the Garvey people and movement a *profound* secret, so much so I am writing you with my own hands, instead of having my stenographer do it... If it is known there that we are doing this...our way will be blocked, and Mr. Garvey, his movement, the U.N.I.A. and myself will be defeated...

Now here is what we want you to do for us.

Make some arrangement to take up the First Mortgage and pay off the pressing judgements by April the 9th and give us time, say Ninety Days, to take the papers out of your hands. By that time the U.N.I.A. will be in a position to handle the matter nicely and blessing and glory will come to you and your group...Now I am writing you from my heart to your heart—*confidentially*, and strictly so, because I believe you to be a friend of Marcus Garvey's and his Race Purity Movement. I have read your speech in Mr. Garvey's "Philosophy and Opinions"...and I am in hearty accord...To come to the help of the U.N.I.A. and Marcus Garvey in this matter right there in Va. will be more than signifi-cant and will be one of the greatest achievements of your life...Praying that God will use your Assoc. and you to help...Marcus Garvey, his ideas, his inter-ests, and millions of Negroes...as well as helping the white race to keep pure...I have the pleasure to be, dear Sir—

Your most humble servant
Caleb G. Robinson.

Robinson actually closed his letter with a P.S. in which he made another appeal to Powell to keep his request a "deathly secret." His pleas, however, would have no effect on the handling of his correspondence. When his letter arrived in Richmond John Powell was away on a concert tour. The letter was read by Miss Louise Burleigh who supported Powell in matters both musical and racial. She later became his wife. When he was away for extended periods she handled his mail and reported to him the happenings in Richmond. It was she then, who first read Robinson's letter. She forward the letter along with the following notation written on March 31, 1926:

You will observe, dearest, how strictly I respected the 'personal' on the enclosure and a good thing I was so revolutionary, too, for I wrote at once to the man and informed him that you were in the West—not saying, however, that I had read the letter, but merely addressing [the note to him by] the street and number!—and [saying] that any reply from you before the first of May was out of the question. After due consideration, I decided against a real answer to the letter...[one that would have explained] the lack of financial resources of the [Anglo-Saxon Clubs of America] etc., because he seemed so very secret about it all that I wondered whether he was quite sane! However, I imagine he is, and I hope that he and his Garveyites will get their school.

I could find no evidence in the John Powell Collection that he ever responded to Caleb Robinson. I have also been unsuccessful in finding out much concerning Robinson's efforts to save the college at Claremont and convert it into a training ground for the 'Back to Africa' movement. Even historical researchers working with the National Park Service just across the James River at Jamestown knew nothing of the existence of a college there when I inquired. Apparently the college and Caleb Robinson's dream died, and even the memory of the institution drifted into obscurity.

Marcus Garvey and his vision of an "Africa for Africans" fared little better. In 1927 Garvey's sentence was commuted by President Coolidge. His release was undoubtedly influenced by Powell and other influential white people who relished Garvey's separatist rhetoric. Dr. W. A. Plecker, Registrar of Vital Statistics in Virginia, an associate of Powell's on race issues, and someone I will have much to say about later, wrote a letter to President Coolidge in March, 1927 which was probably one among many.

To the President,
Washington, D.C.

Sir:

I learn that the application of Marcus Garvey for pardon, and release from Federal Prison at Atlanta, is to be presented to you shortly by the Department of Justice.

I am one of a considerable number of white people in Virginia who have given his case thought, and who believe that his violation of the law was an error of judgment rather than deliberate crime.

Believing that he has been imprisoned sufficiently long to serve the ends of justice, I plead in his behalf that he may be pardoned, and permitted to continue his work with his race in this country.

One of Garvey's chief aims is to inspire his people with the desire to preserve their racial purity, and to teach them abhorrence of mongrelization as it is progressing in the South in spite of restrictions as to intermarriage, and in other sections at a more rapid rate, because of the lack of such restrictions.

Trusting that his application may receive your favorable consideration, I have the honor to be

Most respectfully yours,

W. A. Plecker

Following his release from prison, however, Marcus Garvey was deported as an undesirable alien. He returned to Jamaica and little was ever heard of him again in the United States. In 1934 he moved to London, where he died, virtually unknown and unremembered, in 1940.

References

Burleigh, Louise, (1926), March 31 letter to John Powell, John Powell Collection, Alderman Library, University of Virginia.

Cronon, Edmond D., (1969), *The Story of Marcus Garvey and the Universal Negro Improvement Association*, Madison: The University of Wisconsin Press.

Dabney, Thomas L., (1925), March 12 letter to John Powell, John Powell Collection, Alderman Library, University of Virginia.

Garvey, Marcus, (1923), "An Appeal to the Soul of White America," in Garvey-Jacques, Amy (Editor), (1982), *Philosophy and Opinions of Marcus Garvey*, New York: Antheneum.

Garvey, Marcus, (1925), "The ideals of two races: A message to the negroes of Harlem introducing Mr. John Powell of the Anglo-Saxon Clubs of America, October 28, 1925," in Garvey-Jacques, Amy (Editor), (1982), *Philosophy and Opinions of Marcus Garvey*, New York: Antheneum.

Plecker, W. A., (1927), March 19 letter to the President, John Powell Collection, Alderman Library, University of Virginia.

Powell, John, (1925), "An answer to the appeal to white America: Speech delivered by Mr. John Powell of the Anglo-Saxon Clubs of America at Liberty Hall, New York City on the 28th day of October in Garvey-Jacques, Amy (Editor), (1982), *Philosophy and Opinions of Marcus Garvey*, New York: Antheneum.

Powell, John, (1925), August 25 letter to *The Negro World*, John Powell Collection, Alderman Library, University of Virginia.

Powell, John, (1925), September 15 letter to Thomas Dabney, John Powell Collection, Alderman Library, University of Virginia.

Robinson, Caleb, (1926), March 26 letter to John Powell, John Powell Collection, Alderman Library, University of Virginia.

CHAPTER FOUR

John Powell, Hampton Institute and the Issue of Racial Equality

Hampton Institute has a long and proud history among the predominantly black colleges and universities in the United States. It was founded during the Reconstruction period by General Samuel Chapman Armstrong. Armstrong, a white man, had been given the assignment by the Freedmen's Bureau to help solve the problems being encountered by the thousands of former slaves in Virginia's peninsula region. He was twenty-nine years old when he founded the institution in 1868. Some of the money for the original buildings at the college was raised by a student choir called the Hampton Singers who toured northern communities with Armstrong. He was the son of missionaries, and, as a result, was probably knowledgeable about both choir music and fund raising. Among its distinguished graduates Hampton boasts Booker T. Washington, the gifted black leader and founder of Tuskegee Institute. For over thirty years Hampton also served an important role in the education of Native Americans. Beginning in 1878 federal funds were provided to help support study there by American Indians. Hampton's contribution to the education of this group continued through 1923.

As was noted earlier, one of the prized legislative achievements of John Powell and the Anglo-Saxon Clubs of America was the passage in 1926 by the Virginia General Assembly of a bill requiring the segregation by race of people attending theaters and other places of public assembly. The law was a logical extension of the Race Integrity Act of 1924 in that it was a move toward ever increasing separation of the races. In a sense it was a step toward what might be termed "social purity" whereas the 1924 law had been focused on the "blood purity" of the white race. To understand the law and its timing, however, it is necessary to understand an incident in 1925 involving Hampton Institute.

On March 15 of that year an editorial entitled "Integrity of the Anglo-Saxon Race" appeared in the *Newport News Daily Press*. The editorial charged that nearby Hampton Institute was teaching and practicing "social equality between the white and negro races." While that charge may not seem to be inflammatory in our contemporary context, "social equality" was a catch phrase for white separatists and supremacists for race mixing and all the evils that implied for them. The editorial was written by Walter Scott Copeland, the editor and publisher of the newspaper. He charged that Hampton stood for social equality, that social equality would lead to amalgamation (reproductive mixing) of the races and that "amalgamation would mean destruction of the Anglo-Saxon race in America...[and rather than that we should] prefer that every white child in the United States were sterilized and the Anglo-Saxon race left to perish in its purity."

According to Richard Sherman in his 1987 article entitled "The 'Teachings at Hampton Institute'," the appearance of Copeland's editorial may have been encouraged by a meeting two days earlier in Newport News. The purpose of the meeting was to organize a local chapter of the Anglo-Saxon Clubs of America. John Powell apparently spoke at the meeting and he had a profound influence on Mrs. Copeland, the editor's wife, concerning the "negro problem." Powell's remarks evidently caused Mrs. Copeland to reflect on an evening several weeks earlier when she attended a performance of a group called the Denishawn Dancers at Ogden Hall on the Hampton Institute campus. Sherman cites documents which indicate that Mrs. Copeland felt uncomfortable during the performance because she was seated near black people. A curious complaint, from our perspective today, for someone to make when attending an event at an all black institution. She was apparently incensed, however, that white people had been sold tickets to the performance and then "mixed" in social and physical proximity with black people in the auditorium.

Almost a year later another account of the evening at Ogden Hall was given by Henley Guy, the Secretary and Treasurer of the newly formed Hampton Anglo-Saxon Club. Guy gave an apologetic yet graphic story of his attendance at the dance concert.

> I was guilty of going to Ogden Hall the night of the Denishawn dancers, but hope never to do so again. I saw something there which I believe if the same would be pictured in the mind of each senator [Guy was writing in an effort to lobby support for the social separation bill] they would unanimously support [the bill]. What I saw was a beautiful white woman who had all the appearance of a cultured woman, who would grace any occasion. She was sitting beside a very prominent negro man in front of where I was standing and they smilingly carried on a mutual conversation during the whole performance. It is through this medium the racial barriers can be broken down much more readily than under ordinary circumstances. We want this law on the statute books to compel people of this type from helping to pollute others...

The genesis of Virginia's law requiring separation of the races in public places, then, was the discomfort that a white woman felt in being seated close to black people at a concert at an all black college and the disapproval of a race separatist attending an event at a black college to a conversation between a white woman and a black man. Copeland continued to push the issue and in an editorial in his newspaper on March 20 he printed a letter from James E. Gregg, the principal (president) of Hampton. Gregg's letter was a response to the first editorial and stated that Hampton had never encouraged the "social mingling of the races which would lead to embarrassment on either side." He explained that the policies and actions of the institution had been aimed only at being "courteous and fair" to both the black and white communities. In a seemingly conciliatory voice he said, "I cannot imagine that any thoughtful person could advocate the amalgamation of widely diverse races."

Copeland continued the editorial by posing a number of questions to Dr. Gregg. He asked if it were not true that black and white faculty members meet upon socially equal terms at the college. He asked, "Do they not on occasion sit together at the same table?" He continued, "Are not the students of Hampton Institute taught that the negro race is in all respects the equal of the white race and that no racial distinctions should be made either in law or society?" Copeland charged that a belief in social equality would ultimately lead to race mixing and that the teaching of equality was therefore immoral and an insult to the time-honored customs of Virginia.

Dr. Gregg did not respond to Copeland's questions. Answers did come, however, from a third party. Copeland's rhetoric came to the attention of W. E. B. DuBois and he responded vigorously. DuBois was one of the key figures in the unfolding of post slavery black history in America. He was a prolific writer, a respected social scientist and a pioneering civil rights activist. He was also one of the founders of the N.A.A.C.P. DuBois disagreed strongly with Booker T. Washington's philosophy that black people should stay away from political involvement and concentrate on vocational and economic advancement. He also dismissed Garvey's arguments for separatism, acceptance of inequality and eventual migration to Africa. DuBois believed that black people could only achieve the place they deserved in the American system through political and social action.

DuBois challenged black people to refute the racial stereotypes which continued to enslave even their own thinking about themselves. A primary conduit for his challenges was *The Crisis*, the N.A.A.C.P.'s journal. His editorials in *The Crisis* regularly called for black people to examine the assumptions that others held about them and that they harbored about themselves. In a May 1914 editorial which was cited in a 1981 article by Carol Taylor in the *Journal of Black Studies* he asserted:

> For now nearly twenty years we have made of ourselves mudsills for the feet of this Western world. We have echoed and applauded every shameful accusation made against the 10,000,000 victims of slavery. Did they call us inferior half-beasts? We nodded our simple heads and whispered: 'We is.' Did they call our women prostitutes and our children bastards? We smiled and cast a stone at the bruised breasts of our wives and daughters. Did they accuse of laziness 4,000,000 sweating, struggling laborers, half paid and cheated of much of that? We shrieked: 'Ain't it so?' We laughed with them at our color, we joked at our sad past, and we told chicken stories to get alms.

Dubois abhored the scientific racism of the eugenics movement and he regularly challenged it through his writing and public speeches. He spoke of the social equality of the races as a denied reality and of scientific claims for racial inequality as resulting from flawed and biased science. Carol Taylor discusses Dubois's battle against scientific racism in her article and includes this summation:

> ...In other words, if the Negro was not as American science defined him, then American society's treatment of him was unconscionable. And, DuBois argued, scientific definitions were illogical and unsupported assumptions of a closed system, derived from a laughable methodology , and interpreted by biased investigators. Blacks were not what American science said they were (p. 459).

DuBois answered Walter Copeland's questions about social equality through an editorial in *The Crisis*. The editorial was published in June of 1925. To Copeland came the answer from DuBois: "Yes, we do practice social equality at Hampton. We always have and we always shall. How else can teacher and taught meet but as equals?" Social equality results, said DuBois, in "fine friendships, real knowledge of human souls, high living and high thinking." DuBois' editorial enraged Copeland and others of his ilk, public statements condemning "social equality" were made, and calls for action began to be voiced.

John Powell's voice was heard loudly and often on the issue. He apparently attempted to use his connection with Marcus Garvey in this regard and was accused of pitting one group of black people against another in a manipulative manner. In a letter to *Negro World* on August 25 he said:

> One other matter needs clarification; it has been charged that I have involved Marcus Garvey in an attack on Hampton Institute. This charge is false. I have made no attack on Hampton Institute. I did attempt to induce Dr. Gregg to reply to certain charges which had been brought against the institution. In a letter I wrote him, which was carried by the Richmond papers, I stated that Garvey and the U.N.I.A., would approve all efforts toward the preservation of racial integrity. Garvey's name was mentioned in no other connection.

Richard Sherman's excellent article on the Hampton incident describes a meeting of the Anglo-Saxon Club of Hampton which was held on November 27, 1925. John Powell, Earnest Cox and Walter Copeland each addressed the meeting. The organization then adopted a resolution in protest of the teaching of "social equality" at Hampton and the integrated seating of black and white people at its public assemblies. The group also requested that Delegate George Massenburg of Hampton introduce at the next session of the General Assembly a bill requiring segregated seating at all public gatherings in Virginia. On January 20, 1926 Massenburg introduced the bill in the House of Delegates.

John Powell and his associates in the Anglo-Saxon Clubs were the most active lobbyists for the bill. Henley Guy, the secretary and treasurer of the Hampton chapter, prepared a letter for the members of the Virginia Senate

Illustration 5: Photograph of W.E.B. DuBois. Courtesy of the Archives of the University Library, University of Massachusetts at Amherst.

soliciting support for the bill. Excerpts illustrate the tact being taken to garner backing for the act.

> This question is not local, it is nation wide. Hampton Institute sets a precedent for negro activities all over the world. It is no doubt that the indifference [Hampton] has taken towards this question has been interpreted by the Association for the advancement of the negro race [N.A.A.C.P.] as a tacit approval of their policy of social equality.
>
> I agree with a prominent editor in his idea that if we should place ourselves on a level with negroes at Ogden Hall there would be some radical people who would extend the same courtesies and considerations elsewhere, thus breaking down that public conscience which controls our actions more than anything else. And if anyone should be so fanatical as to invite a colored person in to his home it surely follows that the negro's wife has the same liberty to call on the white man's wife as well as the negro's son to call on the white man's daughter.
>
> ...If the Massenburg bill is defeated it might be construed by people in other states that we sanction mixing of the races...The separation of the races is something inherently deep in the blood of the Southern man and is one of our time honored traditions which is in perfect harmony with this proposed law and if not passed will surely at some time lead to trouble.

The bill was, of course, not without its detractors. Both black and white voices were heard in opposition to it in various parts of the state. One of the most influential opponents was Mary Branch Munford of Richmond. Her deceased husband had been on the board of trustees of Hampton and she was on the board of Fisk University, another black institution. When John Powell learned of Mrs. Munford's opposition to the bill he wrote a letter to her expressing his concern. At best the letter has the flavor of arrogance, at worst it sounds threatening.

> I have learned with grief and dismay of your efforts to defeat the Massenburg bill, and am taking the liberty of bringing to your attention certain grave aspects of the case, which I am sure you have overlooked. Last autumn the situation had grown so serious at Hampton that Major Cox and I went there to try to allay the friction and animosity which were threatening grave and tragic results. A large mass meeting was held, under the auspices of the Hampton post of the Anglo-Saxon Clubs. The grievances of the community against Hampton Institute were brought out. The atmosphere was charged with dynamite. The basis of our organization is good sportsmanship and fair play and respect for law and order. We assured the community that no good results could come from violence and disorder, and that, if they would remain calm, we would present their grievances to the General Assembly and urge that redress be accorded them through the proper legal channels...The opposition to the bill, which is being developed in the Senate, has astounded the citizens of Hampton...They do not believe that the opponents of the bill advocate mixed audiences in places of public entertainment, but they are convinced that the opposition will be so understood by the negroes, within and without the state, and will serve as an incitement to further attacks on the color line...In all seriousness, I warn you that the defeat of this bill may bring tragedy and horror upon the oldest English-speaking community in America.

And lest you think this view exaggerated, let me call to your attention the fact that it is shared by the most level-headed and conservative citizens of Hampton...

I am thoroughly familiar with the situation, and I tell you in all calmness that I do not envy the opponents of this bill the responsibility they are unnecessarily and gratuitously assuming. I beg of you that you believe that this letter is inspired by no impertinent officiousness, nor by exaggerated apprehension, but by a sincere desire to spare you bitter regret.

Mrs. Munford's opposition to the bill was unchanged by Powell's letter and she continued to work actively against it. She and many other Virginians felt the act would be a needless irritant to race relations and that it was an alienating embarrassment to Hampton Institute. She worked with William Howard Taft, who was then Chief Justice of the Supreme Court and was president of the board of trustees of Hampton in trying to defeat the measure. Their efforts were not effective. The bill passed in the House of Delegates on February and in the Virginia Senate on March 9.

John Powell and the Anglo-Saxon Clubs won a contrived power play through the Massenburg bill. They took a trivial matter, an ill founded claim of social mixing of the races, and inflamed and inflated it. They distorted the issue of seating patterns at Hampton's auditorium and made this appear to be an example of a sinister movement toward race amalgamation. They presented the term "social equality" as a threat and rallied support against it. They placed an outrageous and insulting restriction on the lives of all Virginians and established a very negative precedent. Finally, they did personal damage to a number of people, and they discredited and discouraged an important institution of higher education.

During the seating controversy, the charges that Hampton was teaching something akin to race mixing, and the debate over the Massenburg bill, James Gregg was never able to communicate clearly and forcefully about what was being said of his school. Because of varied political and practical reasons, and likely some personal ones as well, he was simply not heard on many of the allegations against Hampton and its policies. Gregg was a white man, Hampton's board of trustees was white, and the institution depended on influential white people for most of its political and financial support. Hampton Institute was a school for black students, controlled by white people and being attacked by another group of white people. Given the circumstances, it is entirely comprehensible that Dr. Gregg's voice was muffled and that the actions of the institution at this time of crisis were slow and awkward.

It is also understandable that the events of 1925 and 1926 would have a very disheartening impact on the faculty and student body of Hampton. In fact, it would have been very unusual if the Hampton Institute community had not become demoralized and angry. This must have been the source of a least part of the frustration which erupted at the college the next year. In October of 1927 a student strike occurred. Two letters in the correspondence of W. E. B.

DuBois provide some insight on the strike and the concerns underlying it. The first was written by a student who remained anonymous.

Dear Sir:

Just a word of a very serious matter here at Hampton. The school is in a very critical situation.

We the students have been wronged, wronged. Yesterday we struck. No inspection, no church, no grace at dinner. At chapel we refused to show off before some Governor from Europe.

The whites are bewildered at the sudden actions of the 'Southern Negroes.' They know not how to act toward the situation. No classes whatsoever today. We have a strong committee of twenty bold, honest upright men pleading for just-Justice, Justice. Ah, if you only knew half. The future of the Negro youth depends upon the results of this serious uprising. Would like for you to help us before we 900 are sent away out in the world.

...We must stick. The officials [are] praying that such will not leak out but please let our mothers, fathers and our race know.

Sincerely,
A loyal Hamptonian (p. 360).

The second letter came from Louise A. Thompson. Miss Thompson was a young teacher in her first year on the faculty at Hampton. In order to appreciate the meaning of the following excerpts from her long letter it is important to remember that the faculty at Hampton was composed of both black and white teachers. How curious it must have been to have had legally mandated segregation between teachers according to race at a school for black students.

As I stated in the beginning, I have not attempted to give you a detailed account of this affair. I shall await your observations on what I have said and what you have learned through other sources...The conciliatory steps taken by some of the white teachers have been most amusing. They threw aside the protecting garment of the Massenberg Bill and the wife of the most prejudiced leader on the campus, whose home is never open to any but the white teachers, sponsored auto parties to take girls to Yorktown, some thirty miles away. Other white-haired ladies wandered around with checker boards, organized sewing bees, gave teas in their rooms, pop-corn parties, and other rather silly amusements as a sop. They cannot realize that there has been a fundamental upheaval which cannot be appeased by simple pastimes. Many pled with tears in their eyes to no avail, for the girls laughed in their faces. They cannot understand that these students for whom they have sacrificed their lives to civilize, in the meantime receiving very comfortable salaries and living quarters which they might have difficulty in securing elsewhere, could feel anything but the deepest respect and gratitude toward them. The teachers as a body do not understand these Negro students, the Administrative Board does not understand them, Dr. Gregg does not understand them—and the tragedy is that they never will. I have found a few, a very few white people who believe in the ideal for which Hampton is supposed to stand, but whose faith has been deeply shaken by this whole affair. As a friend said to me the other day [I assume in reference to the integrated faculty]: 'I believe that interracial experiments will always fail, not because of the impossibility to effect them, but because we cannot be careful enough in the selection of representatives of each side.'

Especially in the Trade School [of Hampton], I learn that there are many inferior white men, some members of the Ku-Klux, who are steeped in southern prejudices. On the other hand, I have witnessed the action of some of the Negro teachers and workers who are just as deadly enemies...Dr. Gregg at a workers meeting last evening issued an ultimatum to workers...He told us that he had been made aware that there were those among us who were student sympathizers and such persons were not wanted at Hampton...Loyalty on the part of the teachers in the present administration is...necessary...and those who felt that they cannot back up the present policies were politely asked to get out (pp. 362–363).

A letter in the John Powell Collection provides a different perspective on Dr. Gregg, his commitment to the institution and his style of action. It also illustrates what may have been Gregg's manner of dealing with the Anglo-Saxon Clubs and other racist forces. Of course this is only one piece of evidence but it does provide a different view of the man.

The letter was written by George Mallison of the Town of Hampton. He was writing to Powell concerning a manuscript he had been working on and for which he was seeking a publisher. The manuscript concerned the "Negro question." Mallison asked Powell to read his manuscript for "grammatical errors and faulty expression." He refers in his letter to several pages in the manuscript which he devoted to the Hampton "situation" and he wanted to be sure he had not "exaggerated the situation or made any misstatements."

The letter indicates that the Hampton chapter of the Anglo-Saxon Clubs had been disbanded, and Mallison blames the disbanding on political and economic pressure generated by Dr. Gregg. He portrays Senator Harry Holt of Hampton as being cooperative with Gregg. He also says that Homer Ferguson, president of the Newport News Shipbuilding and Dry Dock Company, and Frank Darling, a prominent citizen of the area and a trustee of Hampton, were conspirators in the demise of the organization.

The Hampton Anglo-Saxon Club was, to the best of my belief, killed because the politicians quietly passed the word around that this should be done. I understand that Professor Gregg threatened to close at once the Negro primary school he is running [forcing the local government to operate its own school?], and that the institution [Hampton] further threatened to withdraw its money from the banks and cease trading in the town. There has developed what seems to be a 'conspiracy of silence,' making it very difficult to find out anything. However, it appears to me that the conditions in the school and in the Community are worse than they were before the segregation bill was passed. At the recent primary I supported the candidate opposed to Harry Holt (the Boss) and stated on every occasion the opportunity presented itself that I did this because I held Holt responsible for killing the Hampton Club. It did no good. Darling, Ferguson, and [Hampton Institute] run the Peninsula, and Holt and his ilk are subservient to these interests in the end. Holt supported our bill [The Massenburg bill] only because the politicians were smoked out by the passage of the bill in the House and he thought he might loose prestige if he remained quiet.

Illustration 6: Photograph of Dr. James Gregg. Courtesy of Hampton University Archives.

The dissolution of the Hampton Anglo-Saxon Club must have been disturbing to Henley Guy, the previously mentioned secretary and treasurer of that group. It was perhaps confirming to him of what he expressed earlier in his letter to members of the Virginia Senate:

> Some say it is a disgrace to...Virginia to have to pass a law to keep white people from going to colored entertainments but it will be further disgrace if such a law is defeated...thereby giving the cue to DuBois (negro editor) and his white niggers to resume their campaign for social equality in Virginia and if in Virginia, the entire South, and if the South, the entire United States will be involved. It seems that Virginia has been the battle ground for everything in this country.

The image of John Powell as a man having the best interests of both the black and white races is simply not convincing. That was the portrayal of himself that he presented in his private correspondence and public statements concerning Marcus Garvey and the Universal Negro Improvement Association. I have become convinced, however, that the respect he professed for the black race and the support he offered Marcus Garvey were simply manipulative efforts. What he and his colleagues really wanted was to make the United States "pure white" by shipping black people, those for whom freedom from the previously controlling structure of slavery had become so problematic to Powell and his associates, back to Africa. Ideas of social equality, of a respected, truly free and competent black citizenry were anathema to him. I believe that John Powell literally perceived the world in black and white terms. He came from a long tradition of viewing people as belonging in separate social niches on the basis of race, family background, religion, economics and social class. The idea that the barriers separating these niches were breaking down was threatening to Powell. In his struggle to keep the barriers in place he saw people as being either clearly with him or against him, there were no gradients of belief or action from his perspective. He acted forcefully on the basis of his perception of who were his allies and who were his enemies. His memory of those he believed to be his enemies was long lasting and unrelenting. Such was his feeling of resentment toward Hampton Institute.

In March of 1929 the president of the Virginia Federation of Music Clubs wrote to Powell concerning his upcoming appearance at the group's state convention. Annabel Buchanan was an ardent admirer and supporter of John Powell, and over the years they became good friends. In 1929, however, she apparently did not know him well enough to be aware of the depth of his negative feelings about Hampton. She also does not seem to have been aware that there was no rational separation for Powell between the musical and political spheres of his life. Mrs. Buchanan asked for approval from Powell for a matter which she apparently thought was more musical than racial:

> Mr. Powell, do you object to our having the Hampton Choir, with Nathaniel Dett Director, or think it unwise for us to have them in Fredericksburg? I had planned to have them, had written them, and everybody is anxious to have them that I've talked to about it, except Mrs.

Brockenbrough [John Powell's sister], who advised me most strongly against having them—I don't know why, unless it is for racial reasons. They sang for us at Sixth District meeting at Smithfield last fall, coming at their own expense. They sang recently at Norfolk, and I enclose Douglas Gordon's review of their concert. They affected me about as they did him, and the soprano he mentions (not the typical negro treble, which the others all have) has the loveliest voice I've heard in Virginia. Mrs. Brockenbrough said he [Gordon] wrote a 'most biased review' of their concert in Norfolk a year or two ago—I didn't read that, but see nothing biased about this, except that he quite evidently was carried away with them, as others were. I'm aware of the racial disturbances in Hampton, but do not see what they would have to do with our bringing them to Fredericksburg—all they will do will be to come and sing on [the] afternoon program, then go immediately back to Hampton the same day. Our Federation is trying to bring to the attention of the state all the sincere musical work being done in the state—and that is eminently sincere—I've heard them recently and I know how they sing—and artistic. If negros can do work like that, with the choral work we're trying to put over in the state and the interest we are trying to arouse, that should be a inspiration to the white people!

...Of course everyone knows your views on racial integrity, but I suppose all of us agree with you—[but] we want them as negro singers and earnest musical students. I had written them, after Mrs. Brockenbrough's advice, that we could not engage them after all, but am keen on having them, and if you approve, shall wire them to see if they can come on anyway!

...The whole thing is up to you. If you don't want them, they stay off. I think you'd be fair about them. If it were simply a question of prejudice to negro singers, I wouldn't consider that at all—we'd owe it to our negro musicians to pay some attention to what they are doing, especially when they're doing considerably better choral work than anybody else in Virginia, with the possible exception of one or two choruses—certainly better than any of the colleges. I've heard nearly every college chorus in Virginia this past year, and many of the others. It's the racial question I think you'd be concerned over, and that is why I am putting it up to you.

I was unable to locate a copy of Powell's response to Annabel Buchanan's letter. I assume that his response to her was written by hand and, therefore, no copy is included in his papers. Another letter from Mrs. Buchanan, however, makes it clear that Powell refused to have the Hampton choir perform at the same convention where he was appearing. It should be remembered that this was four years after the beginning of the Hampton "incident." Obviously Mrs. Buchanan had not understood when she wrote the letter appealing for the appearance of the choir on the basis of their artistic merits the strength of Powell's resentment toward Hampton Institute. She probably was not aware either of the intensity of his belief in the racial separation of people regardless of common interests, talents and endeavors. On March 26 Annabel Buchanan wrote to Powell saying, "I was both amused and delighted at your speedy response to my special delivery letter. I am disappointed at not having the Hampton Choir; but after all, John Powell is 'the compulsory'. And besides, (perhaps anticipating some such reaction on your part!) I had thoughtfully

---

filled up the entire convention program, so perhaps it is just as well they are not coming."

The race integrity movement was consistently portrayed by its proponents as a struggle by white people against the encroachment upon the purity of their race by black people. The only positive portrayal of black people by white separatists was through their support of the geographical separation and social resignation by black people advocated by Marcus Garvey. An anonymous letter sent to John Powell in March of 1926, however, presents a different, and often unspoken, facet of the race mixing question. It was obviously written with frustration at the publicity being given the issue of race integrity and the characterization of black people as aggressors against white "purity." It is presented here as it was written.

Mr. Powell

In all your propaganda regarding racial relation it appears that you are aiming to vindicate the white man.

In the days of slavery in America, white men forced Negro women to bed with them. If they resisted or resented they were flogged, or sold.

The same rule is in force today, only in a different way. Colored women have to work in private families...hotels and other such places.

In many places when a Negro girl or woman is employed the white men plan to get next to the woman. Within one or two day she is asked to cohabitate with by some white man. If she is a respectable girl or woman she refuse and of course is fired.

They have no protection if they report the case to the courts. Many young Negro girls just from school or the country or out town get work in a private family or boarding house. White men at the places pick a time when the maid is alone in some part of the house. Money is offered. If not accepted, sometimes are made drunk and then the dirty work. If she reports to the head of the house or to the police, they don't take her word.

Negro women coming from work at night from the west end section of this city and urban section are annoyed by and learing by white men. Now all colored women are not common, and want white men or their money.

Of course white men, and official of city government will not see these thing nor will they believe it. The white man is more eager for colored women then the Negro man is for white women. Why make the Negro the goat for all base argument. We are just as good as any race or nationality on the globe.

White men started this mixed color, and they are try to keep at it by using racial integrity as a veil to protect them, and at the same time defile our race. If a white man insults a Negro woman on the street and a Negro man aim to protect her, the Negro man is arrested, some charge placed against him, fined or put in jail.

Is it fair?

Indeed, was it fair? On the envelope in which this unsigned letter was sent was written an apparent comment on its contents. After reading the letter Powell, or someone who previewed it for him, wrote "This needs no answer!" But then, perhaps as an afterthought on the reality of the message of the letter, was added "—but I wish I could have one."

In addition to the public campaigns that John Powell waged for the concept of racial integrity, it appears that he also engaged in personal disputes concerning the words and actions of individuals relative to race relations. Two incidents will serve to illustrate, I believe, that Powell occasionally received reports of what were, according to his code and that of his circle, racially related improprieties. On the basis of these reports he seems to have placed himself in the role of "enforcer" of Anglo-Saxon standards. His vehemence in these actions is apparent in the manner in which he pursued them.

In a letter of August 8, 1924 to Powell, a man named George Peel of Salem, Virginia accused a professor at the Medical College of Virginia of having made a statement that would obviously enrage someone who was devoted to race purity. Peel was following up on a conversation that his sister had earlier with Powell during which she referenced a remark this professor had made in her brother's presence. Peel briefly described the incident:

> In regard to the matter which you spoke to my sister, Miss Alfreda Peel, of a statement which...[professor's name], a former teacher of histology at the Medical College of Virginia made.
>
> To the best of my knowledge this is her statement which she made on the morning of the presidential election. I do not exactly know how this came about but I remember her stating that she would just as soon marry an educated nigger as an illiterate white man.
>
> If you would like to see me about this matter, if you will kindly let me know when you will be in Roanoke...I could meet you at a time and place specified.

Apparently Powell did pursue this matter, and vigorously. Although I have been unable to find any public records of the matter and only two other pieces of correspondence related to it, it is obvious that the issue was pushed.

Dr. Stuart McGuire was president of the Medical College of Virginia at the time of the allegation. McGuire was a man of considerable stature in the medical community of the South and he was held in great civic respect in Richmond. In addition to his leadership of the Medical College of Virginia, he operated his own private hospital, and was known as an outstanding surgeon. He was very active in civic and philanthropic affairs. As is implied in the letter that follows, McGuire must have come to the professor's defense and it appears that he was incensed at Powell's tactics.

The letter was written on January 1, 1925. Powell voices indignation at what he perceived to be the unfair treatment McGuire has afforded him:

Dear Dr. McGuire—

> I was much surprised and pained to learn a few days ago in Philadelphia that you had recently criticized sharply my course in connection with the...affair. Of course, at the time, I realized that you were annoyed with me— you took no pains to conceal your irritation—but I hoped that the eventuation of the affair and your knowledge of my character and associations, would, with the passage of time, establish the fact of my disinterestedness and restore in you amiable feelings toward me. Such, it seems, is not the case. I realize how

fully your time is occupied, nor would I burden your patience for the mere purpose of defending myself. Your opinions and remarks, however, are likely to injure an organization in which I take the deepest interest, which is now carrying out a most useful and necessary work. I refer to the Anglo-Saxon Clubs of America. Consequently, I take the liberty of imposing on your good-nature.

I am not a leader, nor even a member of the Ku Klux Klan. The Anglo-Saxon Clubs are in no way connected with the Klan...

My course in the...affair was not the result of a desire to meddle, but sprang largely from a friendly feeling towards yourself. My effort, on the one hand, was to spare you and your associates the unpleasantness of a scandal, on the other, to save the community from the disgrace of cowardly violence directed against a woman, attended by possible riot and bloodshed.

I never threatened the Medical College nor...[the professor] with the Klan. On the contrary, I placed myself in jeopardy and was exposed to great unpleasantness and annoyance in my attempts to protect your faculty and...[the professor]. I neither desired nor expected thanks, but I must strongly protest against a misconception which would hold me responsible for the very abuses against which I was contending. I find it amazing that such misconception could have arisen in a community with which I have been intimately connected for forty-two years.

I trust that this simple statement may suffice to disabuse your mind of its misconception, but fear that if you should think so ill of me as to hold me capable of threatening a woman with a mob of blackguards, my unsurported [sp.] word will have but small effect. Fortunately, I am in a position to verify by credible witnesses every statement that I have made. I shall be glad to do so, if you are sufficiently interested to give half an hour to the matter.

I must request, however, that you make no repetition of the charges against me, at least, until I have been given opportunity to make you acquainted with the facts in the case.

I shall await an early reply to this letter.

Dr. McGuire's response on January 9 was curt and perfunctory. Apparently he wanted no further dealings or dialogue with Powell.

I have been unusually busy and this is the first opportunity I have found in which to reply to your letter of January 1st, and I must confess I have been unable to give much thought to the subject.

I do not remember having criticised your action in the...affair since the matter was terminated by the teacher's withdrawal from the Faculty. I have certainly made no 'charges' against you.

If you will be more specific and show where I have wronged you in any way, I will be glad to try to make amends.

A second example of Powell's personal battles over issues of race involves Arthur W. James an official with the Virginia Board of Public Welfare. In a letter of June 6, 1925 Powell explained that he had felt negatively toward James since visiting the Welfare Bureau some months earlier. While there he had noticed a copy of a pamphlet entitled "Eugenics and the Racial Integrity Law." The pamphlet was written by Dr. W. A. Plecker, Registrar of Vital Statistics, ardent race separatist, and the main character in the next chapter of this book. Powell commented favorably on the pamphlet. Mr. James apparently countered Powell's remark with a negative comment and added that he thought that Dr. Plecker was using his official position to conduct a campaign of propaganda against black people. Powell claimed he was amazed at this comment, and he defended both Plecker and the pamphlet. He said that the encounter soon left his mind and was not recalled until some time later.

I doubt that the incident really left his mind, however, and I am certain that James came into clear focus when friends reported to Powell comments made at a meeting of the Virginia Board of Censors in May. Apparently Powell himself had been invited to attend the meeting and assist in the judgment of a movie. He could not attend but Earnest Cox and Louise Burleigh did. Arthur James was also present. The movie in question was "The House Behind the Cedars." According to *Frame by Frame: A Black Filmography*, the film was an adaptation of the play by the same title. It is described as the story of a black woman "passing" as white and having a happy ending with her black lover. Obviously this was a film with the potential to be disquieting to some of the people who have been discussed in this chapter.

I was not present at the meeting which passed on 'The House Behind the Cedars.' But I am well acquainted with most of those who were there, several of whom immediately after my arrival in Richmond reported to me the happenings of that morning. The reports I received came to me separately, but were, nevertheless, in agreement, practically to the point of identity. My informants were persons of eminent intelligence, of balanced judgement, impartial and devoid of malice, unusually sensitive to the values of words. I had no reason to doubt their voracity nor their accuracy. Of course, you know best the impression you intended to produce. The impression you actually did produce was that of pained and indignant amazement. This applied to your attitude in general. In particular, you were alleged to have said that you would like to see the leading lawyers, the leading physician, and the leading minister of the Gospel of Richmond, negroes; and that at any time the best citizens of Richmond could be seen at Atlantic City dancing in cabarets with negresses.

The account of your attitude and utterances in the Censors' office recalled to me your opinions about Dr. Plecker's pamphlet. This did not diminish the painful impression already produced. The statements attributed to you had been made on an official, if informal, occasion, nor had your manner indicated any desire on your part that they remain unnoticed. Consequently, I saw no reason to refrain from using the information which had been given me, all the more so, as I felt that such views and expressions on the part of a State official—especially one connected with the Board of Public Welfare, constituted, in the present delicate and tense situation, a very real menace to the public. If you had been a friend, or even an old acquaintance, I should have lost no time in making a protest to you, yourself. As the matter stood, to approach you personally would, I felt, be an impertinence. Freedom of thought, freedom of speech for the individual, are sacred to me. I am the last to wish to bludgeon the views of anyone into conformity with my own. I demand for myself, and shall exercise, the same privileges I accord others. I shall not hesitate to criticise the actions and expressed views of public servants whenever they may seem to me unsound or dangerous, nor shall my criticism, I trust, ever be coloured by personal animus or malicious intent.

Accordingly at the last meeting—which by the way was not a public meeting—of the Virginia Post No. 1, Anglo-Saxon Clubs of America, I brought to the attention of the society the reports about you which I had received. The Post, by unanimous action, appointed a committee...to look into the matter and to take such action as might seem appropriate. Wishing to treat you with all fairness and consideration, the committee sent you a letter dated May 25th. A copy of your reply of May 28th was forwarded to me...and was received on the same mail which brought your personal letter. On reading your reply to the committee, I was much relieved that you had disclaimed the sentiments and expressions attributed to you. I immediately showed your letter to those who had reported to me your alleged statements. I am sorry to have to tell you that they insist upon holding to their original accounts despite your denial. However, they are willing to put their statements in writing over their signatures. I shall send you copies of these statements as soon as possible so that you may have opportunity to explain to them any possible misunderstanding. When you have cleared up the question with them, I shall, of course be happy to make the result as widely known as I can. I have no desire to persecute you or to do you the slightest injustice.

I have stated as frankly as possible my part in this matter. The whole affair, as far as I am concerned, has been entirely impersonal. My sole consideration has been and is the preservation of racial integrity, which in my opinion can only be achieved by the keenest watchfulness and the strictest maintenance of all racial distinctions. If, however, you desire—as your letter intimates—to institute against me a suit for slander, I must tell you without any hesitation that I should welcome the opportunity to clear up before the public a matter so deeply affecting the public welfare.

This letter appears to have been meant to intimidate. It may have worked and a subsequent letter was probably reinforcing of that effect. On July 8 Powell wrote to James that because there was a difference between what James recalled saying and what others recalled, he would be given the opportunity "—which in fairness is due you—to explain the discrepancy between your letter to the Anglo-Saxon committee and the impression they received from the occasion itself." Attached to the letter were the following signed statements from Louise Burleigh and Earnest Cox:

At a meeting at the office of the Board of Censors I heard Mr. Arthur James of the Board of Public Welfare express opinions which created an atmosphere of antagonism in what had been a friendly discussion up to the moment of his entering it, and which seemed to me so opposed to the consensus as to indicate that Mr. James' feeling about the proper position of the races differed fundamentally from that of the other people present and from the accepted standard in Virginia.

In particular, I heard and have remembered two statements Mr. James made: first, in reply to Mrs. Sampson, who told of the cutting of a Fox film to meet the demands of the new Racial Integrity law as interpreted by the Censors, Mr. James said that such an action was quite unnecessary, as 'you can at any time, go up to Atlantic City and see the best people in Richmond dancing in cabarets with negresses;' and second, in speaking of a negro lawyer who was, I understood, known to Mr. James personally and upon friendly terms, Mr. James said that he had written lately to urge that he come to Richmond, adding that for his part he would be glad to see the best lawyer, doctor and minister of the Gospel in Richmond, negroes.

Louise Burleigh.

I will state that in my opinion the general attitude and several specific statements of Mr. Arthur James at the discussion of the propriety of THE HOUSE BEHIND THE CEDARS were not consistent with the historical and conventional southern attitude toward the negro and the negro problem. This is my opinion. Mr. James, by some method, may find it possible to correlate his views with the conventional opinions on the negro problem. He may find this a possibility, but from the impressions that I received it would be a difficult thing to do. I remember very little in detail of the statements he made, but I do recall an expression of his views in relation to wishing an eminent negro lawyer for Richmond. This arose in regard to correspondence which he stated he had recently had with a negro lawyer. I wish to state definitely that I was the one who pointed out that the spirit of the closing scene of the picture under consideration tended to violate the new racial integrity act. I have no desire to enter into controversy, and am giving this simply as a report of the impression created upon me by Mr. James.

Earnest S. Cox.

Parallels have often been drawn between the eugenics movement in the United States and the events which unfolded in Germany during the Nazi regime earlier in this century. I draw several such parallels in this book. Both movements do, indeed, go back to common philosophical roots. There were shared rationales in the race hygiene program in Germany and the involuntary sterilization, institutionalization, and immigration restriction programs in the United States. The arguments for restrictive marriage laws in Germany and those in America are stunningly similar. German and American scientists and policy makers spoke of each other in admiring terms in relation to eugenics. It should come as no surprise then that John Powell was an admirer of the cultural and political programs of the Nazis prior to World War II. It is notable, however, that even after the war when most eugenic enthusiasts had retreated from speaking admiringly of Nazi eugenic programs, Powell persisted, at least to some degree, in his admiration. His niece, Rebecca Brockenbrough, while serving in Europe with the WACs in 1945, wrote regularly to her sister, Elizabeth, concerning the aftermath of the war. Apparently Elizabeth shared some of Rebecca's observations that their Uncle John was persisting in his positive assessment of the Nazis and what they had attempted. On June 13, 1945 Rebecca wrote to Elizabeth and included in her letter:

I think Uncle John is just being argumentative when he calls the Germans 'kindly.' We could take his own nephews and turn them into brutes if we started early enough. For twenty years the old ideals have been ridiculed and spat upon, figuratively speaking, [in Germany] and brute strength, cruelty, and megalomania raised in their stead. Uncle John wouldn't have to come to the concentration camps over here to see the trend—all he need do is talk to the PWs [prisoners of war] over there. I wish he could talk to some of our boys who have seen the victims of torture...If there are many people like Uncle John we'll be doing this again in a few years—and not three thousand miles away from the U.S.

In April of 1928 John Powell and Louise Burleigh were married. For more than a decade they made their home in Richmond, often traveling and performing in Virginia, various parts of the United States and in Europe. Later, however, they bought a mountaintop home near Charlottesville and, even though they spent much time each year in their Richmond home, it eventually became their primary residence. Pocahontas Edmunds, the friend of the Powells who proudly claimed her descendance from the Indian princess, described their home "Longways" in her biographical account of John Powell's life. It provides an ironic glimpse of his later life:

> Fortunately for their comfort, they [the Powells] had a Negro couple, Lydia and John Banks, who lived in a five-room cottage nearby which was built for them by the Powells. They had additional remunerative employment in Charlottesville, and in time bought a new Oldsmobile car for themselves. They did the basic cooking, mending and repairing for the...couple (p. 366).

The extent of the reliance that the Powells put on Lydia and John Banks is evident in a series of letters and notes written to them by Louise and John Powell between 1944 and 1960. The correspondence took place primarily when the Powells were in their Richmond home and the Banks were caring for Longways. Birthday and Easter presents were included with some of the notes, and Louise Powell closed most of her letters with expressions of love for the couple. A letter which is undated but which appears to have been written in the late fifties reveals the trust felt by an aging couple for dependable friends:

> Dear Lydia,
>
> Ophelia is using the Electrolux and I have to write on the dining room table. We are pretty well settled and unpacked.
>
> I think, with help from so many people, we got away from Longways fairly well. I was especially grateful to Banks, who not only was very kind, but knew exactly what had to be done and went about doing it. Everybody else had to ask questions, so my mind was taken off what *I* had to do.
>
> The thing which troubles me now is electric current. I had intended to make sure that the big switch under the porch was pulled out, but so many people were asking me what to do with all sorts of things that I forgot the switch. And when Mr. Powell said the power for the music-room had never been turned off, I began to worry about fire. And in spite of the fact that I talked with you and told you I keep thinking about it. I woke up about seven o'clock, as I have done all summer. I ought to go back to sleep, but do not, instead, I keep wondering about Longways.
>
> This morning I thought that if I knew that switch had been pulled, I would stop the silly worrying...

The letter continued with a request that Lydia confirm for her that the electric switch had been turned off. So John and Louise Powell came to depend in their later years, as most of us have or will, more and more on

Illustration 7: John Powell writing music at his piano. Photograph courtesy of Special Collections, Alderman Library, University of Virginia.

trusted friends for help in the routines of their daily living. Race is not an issue in such relationships. Again, what an irony.

John Powell died on August 15, 1963 at "Longways" of a heart attack. He was eighty years old. In the four column account of his death which was published in Charlottesville's *Daily Progress* the next day no mention was made of Powell's philosophy and activities concerning race. A detailed account of his career as a musician, his accomplishments as a composer and performer, and the honors he received for his musical achievements (including his recognition in 1951 when Governor John Battle declared November 5 as "John Powell Day") was given. Two days after his death the *Richmond Times-Dispatch* printed a tribute to John Powell on its editorial page. The memorial did not refer at all to his social beliefs or political activities. It praised him as a musician. The last sentence of the tribute is probably very accurate. "In personality and character he was truly exceptional, and as a pianist and composer he was unique in the annals of the Old Dominion." He truly was an exceptional individual. The tragedy, however, was that he attempted to impose a cadence and control over other people that was destructive to their lives. While his quest for an ordered sense of purity may have led to beauty in his music, it was a destructive obsession that damaged the lives of people who did not and could not achieve an Anglo-Saxon ideal. John Powell was a gifted artist and musician. When he faced the diversity of humankind, however, he was myopic and intolerant.

References

Anonymous, (1926), March 1 letter to John Powell, John Powell Collection, Alderman Library, University of Virginia.

Aptheker, Herbert, (1973), *The Correspondence of W.E.B. DuBois, Volume I*, Boston: University of Massachusetts Press.

Buchanan, Annabel, (1929), March 23 letter to John Powell, John Powell Collection, Alderman Library, University of Virginia.

_____, (1929), March 26 letter to John Powell, John Powell Collection, Alderman Library, University of Virginia.

Brockenbrough, Rebecca, (1945), June 13 letter to Elizabeth Brockenbrough, Rebecca Brockenbrough Collection, Virginia Military Institute Archives, Lexington, Virginia.

Burleigh, Louise, (no date), Statement concerning Arthur James, John Powell Collection, Alderman Library, University of Virginia.

Copeland, Walter S., (1925), "Integrity of the Anglo-Saxon Race," *Newport News Daily Press*, March 15.

_____, (1925), "Teachings at Hampton Institute," *Newport News Daily Press*, March 20.

Cox, Earnest, (no date), Statement concerning Arthur James, John Powell Collection, Alderman Library, University of Virginia.

DuBois, W.E.B., (1925), "Social Equality at Hampton," *The Crisis*, June, 1925, pp. 59–60.

Edmunds, Pocahontas, (1972), *Virginians Out Front*, Richmond, VA: Whittet and Shepperson.

Guy, Henley, (1926), February letter draft to Virginia senators, John Powell Collection, Alderman Library, University of Virginia.

"John Powell," (1963), *Richmond Times-Dispatch*, August 17, p. 12.

Klotman, Phyllis, (1979), *Frame By Frame: A Black Filmography*, Bloomington: Indiana University Press.

Mallison, George, (1927), October 7 letter to John Powell, John Powell Collection, Alderman Library, University of Virginia.

McGuire, Stuart, (1925), January 9 letter to John Powell, John Powell Collection, Alderman Library, University of Virginia.

Peel, George T., (1921), August 8 letter to John Powell, John Powell Collection, Alderman Library, University of Virginia.

Powell, Louise, (Undated), Letter to Lydia Banks, John Powell Collection, Alderman Library, University of Virginia.

Powell, John, (1925), January 1 letter to Stuart McGuire, John Powell Collection, Alderman Library, University of Virginia.

_____, (1925), June 6 letter to Arthur James, John Powell Collection, Alderman Library, University of Virginia.

_____, (1925), July 8 letter to Arthur James, John Powell Collection, Alderman Library, University of Virginia.

_____, (1925), August 22 letter to *Negro World*, John Powell Collection, Alderman Library, University of Virginia.

_____, (1926), March 5 letter to Mrs. Munford, John Powell Collection, Alderman Library, University of Virginia.

Sherman, Richard, (1987), "The 'Teachings at Hampton Institute' Social equality, racial integrity, and the Virginia Public Assemblage Act of 1926," *The Virginia Magazine of History and Biography*, Vol. 95, No. 3

Taylor, Carol M., (1981), "W. E. B. DuBois's Challenge to Scientific Racism," *Journal of Black Studies*, Vol. 11, No. 4, pp. 449–460.

"Virginia's Leading Composer Dies...," (1963), *Charlottesville Daily Progress*, August 16, p. 13.

CHAPTER FIVE:

W. A. Plecker, Vital Statistics and the Color Line

The title of the act that John Powell and his colleagues created and lobbied so actively for, and which was passed in the General Assembly of Virginia in 1924, was "An Act to Preserve Racial Integrity." The title is a misnomer. The law in reality only provided for the "racial integrity" of white people. The law prohibited the intermarriage of the Caucasian race with any other race or any person of any traceable mixture of races. The one exception was that persons with one-sixteenth or less of American Indian ancestry were considered "white" under the law. As was mentioned earlier, this exception was an appeasement to those old Virginia families who had long boasted of their "noble" Indian links. With this exception all other people were barred from marriage with whites. Specifically the law's language noted that the following groups were prohibited: "Negroes, Mongolians, American Indians, Malayans, or any mixtures thereof, or any other non-Caucasic strains." It did not prohibit these races or groups from intermarrying with one another. In essence the law did not address racial integrity, it dealt only with white racial integrity. The law, in effect, created two racial groupings: white and everyone else.

Originally proposed as part of the act was a clause that would have provided for statewide ancestral registration. In other words, every resident of Virginia would have to register as to his or her race on the basis of ancestral evidence. This registration would then be used at the time a marriage application was made and this would prevent the "passing" of "mulattoes" and other "mixtures" into the white race. The *Virginia Pilot and Norfolk Landmark*, even though supporting antimiscegenation legislation, described the provision in these terms:

> ...each person, not already booked in the Vital Statistics Bureau will be required to take out a sort of passport correctly setting forth his racial composition 'in so far as ascertainable'...without such a passport, though this racial identity be as clear as crystal, he will not be able to obtain a license to marry of his own kind...Virginia can afford to have nothing to do with this preposterous scheme to force the whole population, those already married, those not married, as well as those past the age of marriage, to take out passports attesting their racial composition, in order that a documentary check may be had on

the one or two per cent of the population so indefinitely blooded and pigmented as to need registration.

Enough opposition eventually developed to the registration provision that it was eliminated as a compulsory feature of the act. Registration was left optional so that persons who wished to have their race and ancestry established officially could do so through a formal application procedure. There would not prove to be many takers of this "opportunity."

The person who assisted John Powell in all of his racial integrity efforts and who was most assuredly the author of the original compulsory registration provision of the race integrity law was Dr. Walter Ashby Plecker. As State Registrar of Vital Statistics, Plecker was in a strategic and powerful position relative to race issues. For years he used his position and influence to promote the agendas of John Powell and the Anglo-Saxon Clubs, and to carry forward his own personal race campaigns. For years he also pursued with vengeful enthusiasm individuals and groups he felt were violating the race integrity laws of Virginia or what he perceived to be the natural laws of racial separation. For decades he appointed himself as judge, jury and executioner when he encountered what he believed were violations of these laws.

Dr. Walter Plecker was born in Augusta County, Virginia in 1861. He graduated from a military secondary school, attended the University of Virginia, and earned his medical degree from the University of Maryland. He did further study in obstetrics at the New York Polyclinic. He practiced for one year in Rockbridge County, Virginia and then moved to Birmingham, Alabama. After practicing for several years in Alabama Plecker moved back to Virginia. In his own words:

> From 1892 to 1910 I was engaged in the practice of medicine in Hampton, Virginia. In 1900 Elizabeth City County [the Hampton area] secured a special enactment of the legislature permitting the establishment of a County Health Department, including the securing of vital statistics of births and deaths. Two or three years later...I was made health officer without supervision or instructions. In order to study the reasons for a colored death rate double that of the white, I determined to spare no effort to secure as near 100% registration of births and deaths, with causes, as possible and believe that it reached not less than 98% completeness. Reports based upon this study attracted the attention of Dr. Ennion G. Williams, then Health Commissioner of the newly established State [Health] Department...In the early part of 1912, I was called...into the Richmond office and assigned the task of aiding in the drafting of a vital statistics bill and securing its passage through the legislature against strong opposition. We were granted an appropriation...I decided to undertake it [directing the new bureau]. I was asked to set my own salary and placed it at one of a little more than subsistence...

On March 13, 1925 Plecker wrote a letter to the editor of a magazine entitled the *Survey Graphic*. He was writing concerning an article which he felt expressed approval of mixed race marriages. He lectured the editor on the ill effects that his magazine's positive portrayal of miscegenation could have on society. In the letter Plecker also demonstrated his romanticized image of a "good negroe."

> Those of us who have been reared with the negroes have attachment for them, at times very warm, even though we know them from every angle.
>
> My own recollection reaches back to the period during the War between the States, when as a young child I was largely under the control of a faithful servant who had been born in my mother's family and was early assigned to her as her personal maid, and went with her when she married and established her own home.
>
> When this maid, Delia, finally married, the ceremony being performed in the home of her colored friend, my young sister broke forth into an outburst of sobbing and was joined by Delia, almost breaking up the wedding.
>
> In my mother's last illness she sent for this faithful servant friend to nurse her, and it was she who closed her eyes after death.
>
> When my mother's will was read we found that Delia was remembered, and as executor the first check I drew was for her.

Plecker also went on in the letter to explain his perception of the need for the race integrity legislation in Virginia that had been enacted the year before. He also made it clear that, even though the mandatory registration provision of the law had been deleted from the final form of the act, he still saw it as part of his "mission" to racially classify the people of the state.

> As much as we held in esteem individual negroes this esteem was not of a character that would tolerate marriage with them, though as we know now to our sorrow much illegitimate mixture occurred.
>
> While we slumbered this illegitimate mating went on and on until we have now in Virginia many thousands of white negroes who until less than a year ago were quietly and persistently passing over the [color] line.
>
> Aroused to the seriousness of the situation and the impending danger the Virginia legislature in 1924 passed a 'Racial Integrity' law defining a white person as one with no trace of other blood, forbidding the marriage of whites and those with the least degree of mixture.
>
> As State Registrar of births and deaths, marriage and divorces, my task of properly classifying our population as to color began—a tremendous one.
>
> ...If you desire to do the correct thing for the negro race join us in the effort to educate our young men as to the crime against the State and both white and colored races when they mix their blood with that of another totally opposite race. Inspire the negroes themselves with the thought that the birth of mulatto children is a standing disgrace. The fact that many negro females and particularly the near-white members of the race, willingly yield to the disgraceful proposals of lustful white men, is a stigma which on its face mark their illegitimate off-spring as undesirable additions to the white race. That in spite of the fact that such offspring may inherit from the father forceful qualities which combined possibly with good ones found in many negroes, enable them to attain positions of prominence in various spheres of life.

It is obvious from this letter that Plecker saw his public office as a vehicle for acting on his philosophy of race and race relations. The degree to which this merging of public and private purposes was true of Plecker will become even more clear later in this and in following chapters. Plecker's zeal will be revealed through letters which were sent as official correspondence by him as the State Registrar but which crackle with his personal vehemence. In some cases I will not use the names of the persons Plecker was writing to and I will delete their names from the reference citation. These people were hurt once by these letters, they and their descendants deserve to be protected today from things that were said irresponsibly in the past.

Just over a month after the race integrity law was enacted Dr. Plecker wrote two letters concerning the recent birth of a child in Lynchburg. He sent copies of this official correspondence to John Powell. Although there could not have been any official justification for sharing this information with Powell, perhaps in his mind it was justified because they were allies in the war for race purity. Whatever his rationale, however, he continued this practice for two decades, sending Powell literally hundreds of copies of correspondence from his office.

At the top of first of the two copies of the letters to Lynchburg Plecker wrote a note in his own hand: "Dear Mr. Powell, This is a specimen of our daily troubles and shows how we handle them."

The first letter is to the mother of a child born the previous summer. Plecker was writing on the basis of a "tip" he had received from a Health Department worker in Lynchburg. The April 30 letter is in no way tentative or exploratory, it is declarative and not investigatory.

> Dear Madam:
>
> We have a report of the birth of your child, July 30th, 1923, signed by _____, midwife.
>
> She says that you are white and that the father of the child is white [at the time midwives could process the form for birth certificates for children they helped deliver].
>
> We have a correction to this certificate sent to us from the City Health Department at Lynchburg in which they say that the father of this child is a negro.
>
> This is to give you warning that this is a mulatto child and you cannot pass it off as white.
>
> A new law passed by the last Legislature says that if a child has one drop of negro blood in it, it cannot be counted as white.
>
> You will have to do something about this matter and see that this child is not allowed to mix with white children. It cannot go to white schools and can never marry a white person in Virginia.
>
> It is an awful thing.

The second letter went to the midwife.

> Dear Madam:
>
> This is to notify you that it is a penitentiary offense to willfully state that a child is white when it is colored. You have made yourself liable to very serious trouble by doing this thing. What have you got to say about it?

Walter Plecker apparently shared information from his office, and his impressions concerning the racial ancestry of people he actually knew little about, with a number of people whom he felt could help advance the cause of race integrity. In July, 1924, R. N. Anderson wrote to Plecker asking for clarification on information cited at a meeting he had attended. Mr. Anderson was a school superintendent in a rural Virginia county and had recently attended an educator's conference where a speaker on race integrity stated that fifty of the most influential families in Mr. Anderson's county had been found to have negro blood; that they were ignorant of the fact themselves and were intermarrying and associating with the best people of the county; and that authorities in the county were afraid to report these cases. Apparently Dr. Plecker was acknowledged as the source of this information. Understandably Mr. Anderson was interested in knowing more about this situation and wrote concerning the accuracy of what he had heard.

In his response Dr. Plecker confirmed having shared information with the speaker, Reid Williams, and made some corrections of particular points. He seems to have had no hesitation in affirming that he was the source of the claims:

> Mr. Williams is very much interested in this matter and comes into my office frequently when he comes to Richmond. He doubtless received information of the mixed families...from me, but evidently did not distinguish accurately the difference between individuals and families. I did not count the number on the list but judge there were 40 or 50 [individuals]. He was of course misled into believing that they had intermarried with influential families, which certainly would not be the case from the origin of them. However, the physician who first called our attention to this was anxious that his name be not announced as it would injure his standing professionally...evidently indicating that some of them are people of some financial standing.
>
> I will send Mr. Williams a copy of this letter that he may avoid falling into a similar error in the future. I have no information except the list of which you are aware.
>
> We are now beginning to get in touch with similar conditions throughout the State and are trying to establish a list of all doubtful families. It is an immense undertaking...Of course, I am up against the question of offending and antagonizing individuals which cannot be avoided. We cannot consider the individual but the State.

Contrary to the affectionate regard for black people which Plecker expressed in his description of his relationship to Delia, his actions seemed to consistently demonstrate a profound disregard for them as free human beings. They are only viewed as acceptable to him in subservient and controlled positions. Plecker reveals what appears to be his honest opinions of black people in a letter to John Gailey on May 21, 1925. Mr. Gailey had read an extract of a speech Plecker made to the American Public Health Association. Gailey was apparently impressed with Plecker's comments and wrote asking that he elaborate on some points made in his address. Dr. Plecker seemed delighted to do so and included the following remarks in his lengthy letter.

> ...As a rule a negro is improvident, easily satisfied, especially if he has the opportunity for sexual relations, and is not dependable. There are few negroes who can resist the temptation to steal, at least in a small way. Before the war

Illustration 8: Photograph of W.A. Plecker from Bruce, Phillip (1924), *History of Virginia*, New York: The American Historical Society, Vol.5, p. 397.

between the States, however, the negro had reached the highest state of development that he has ever reached. Then his faithfulness to his master was one of the most notable things...amongst us of the South. All of this, however, has entirely changed since the new ideas have been introduced from the North and since the horrors of the reconstruction days. His attitude is antagonistic to the white race...This attitude is very greatly increased through the efforts of their mulatto leaders, especially the New York Association for the Advancement of Colored People, who have the endorsement of a certain type of influential and moneyed white people.

...The true negro is probably indifferent to the subject [of race mixing], not having foresight enough to see clearly the significance of it. The inter-mixture has come through their laxness in morals, which is the most controlling motive of their lives. The whole of our trouble comes through the near whites who are striving in every way to pass over into the white class.

Walter Plecker's influence on opinions and race relations extended far beyond the boundaries of Virginia. His reputation grew through his writings and he came to be recognized nationally as an authority on race. As mentioned earlier, his address to the American Public Health Association in 1924 was published the next year as an article in the *American Journal of Public Health*. The article was entitled "Virginia's Attempt to Adjust to the Color Problem" and, of course, dealt primarily with the menace of race mixing. Plecker's *Eugenics in Relation to the New Family* was published in 1925 by the Bureau of Vital Statistics. It was another eugenic warning about the dangers of race mixing and intermarriage. In the introduction it was explained that the booklet was intended for young people in schools and colleges. In 1932 the American Museum of Natural History hosted the Third International Congress of Eugenics. The papers from that meeting were published in a volume entitled *A Decade of Progress in Eugenics*. Plecker's paper, "Virginia's Effort to Preserve Racial Integrity" was included.

Walter Plecker's influence, then, was international in scope. He received requests from across the United States and around the world for information and advice on racial matters. Plecker seemed always ready to respond to these requests, apparently no matter of race was too large or too small for his attention. Among the copies of his letters in the John Powell Collection are responses to requests for help from university professors and foreign scientists. Plecker was quick to offer theoretical perspectives or historical insights on the "race problem." He was also quite willing to become involved in local matters of "who" married "who," of course. But he was also quick to involve himself in "who" went to school "where," and even "who" was buried "where."

Several school superintendents developed a pattern of writing to Plecker concerning children they thought might be of "questionable" race. Plecker maintained a sort of "hit list" of names of people he was convinced were mulattos or, as he referred to them in some correspondence, "near white." If he found the name in question on his list he would advise the superintendent to exclude the children from white schools. The supporting evidence for his lists appears to have been very weak in many cases. In at least one case he advised school exclusion based on no evidence beyond the physical appearance of the children in question. The superintendent of the Pittsylvania County Schools wrote to Plecker concerning four children with fair complexions but with what some people thought were negroid features. The letter also contained a petition from fifteen citizens of the county asking that the children be excluded from white schools. Plecker replied:

> This is the first time that our attention has been called to this family, and we have no information in regard to them. We have, however, made a photostat copy of the petition, which we will preserve in our files as evidence, being the opinion of fifteen citizens of that county, and upon that information we will designate any of these children found in our records as colored regardless of the statement of the attendant who reported these births.

As incredible as it may seem, Dr. Plecker is saying in this letter that he is accepting the "votes" of fifteen people in regard to the race of these children and, on that basis alone, he will alter the official birth records of the children according to those "votes." The July 11, 1940 letter continues:

> The suggestion which we would make is that if these children are definitely negroid in appearance, and especially if one of the parents is known to be colored, they be classified as colored and excluded from the white schools. [No mention is made of on what basis a parent may be 'known to be colored' but it appears that the same kind of 'voting' would suffice]. Of course when they become adult they should not be permitted to intermarry into the white race.

Walter Plecker apparently trained his clerks at the Bureau of Vital Statistics to watch carefully for the names on his lists of people who, according to his belief, were trying to pass as white. It seems probable that they were also made sensitive to other indicators that marriage records or other documents being processed should be brought to his attention. There are numerous copies of letters that Plecker sent to people who had applied for marriage licenses or whose infant's birth certificates were being issued by his office, and whom he accused of attempting to "pass" themselves or their children as white. The letters were usually threatening in tone (Plecker would often mention that a penitentiary term was possible for violators of the law on race integrity). Many of the letters also included a patronizing and scolding statement or two. He also sent letters to local court officials and Commonwealth's attorneys reporting irregularities and urging action. On September 6, 1940, for example, Plecker wrote to the Commonwealth's Attorney in Galax, Virginia:

> Dear Sir:
>
> In our...[records] is a certificate for the birth of a child born March 22, 1940, to _____ and _____. This certificate states that the man is white and the woman, to whom he was married November 11, 1935 in Grayson County, is given as mulatto.
>
> When we wrote Dr. _____ to learn whether the statement that one was white and the other mulatto was an error or correct, he returned

another certificate in which the same facts were stated, that the man is white and the woman mulatto. That being true, they were married illegally and under the laws of Virginia they are not legally married [now]. Both are liable to the State Penitentiary.

That is all the information we have as to the case. We know nothing further to substantiate the facts. I am reporting this to you as Commonwealth's Attorney in order that you may take such action as you may deem necessary.

The degree of Dr. Plecker's zeal for his cause and the extent of his monitoring of records for racial questions is perhaps best illustrated by his correspondence with the superintendent of a cemetery in Charlottesville. Plecker had taken special note of the death certificate of a man who had apparently been on one of his lists. After noticing the date and place of the man's burial he wrote to the superintendent:

> We are under the impression that Riverview Cemetery is reserved for white interments. Possibly you are not aware of the fact that this man is of negro ancestry. The record of this man's birth...shows his mother as colored. Other records of our office confirm this classification. There is a mulatto branch of the white recognition.
>
> We are giving you this information to take such steps as you may deem necessary. You probably know whether the State law permits the use of a white cemetery for colored people.

In a second letter on August 3, 1940 Plecker responded to questions from the Riverview Cemetery's secretary. He apparently had explained that the man in question had been buried in a section of the cemetery set aside for the poor. He must also have told Dr. Plecker that he was unaware of any law which required segregation in cemeteries. Plecker replied, however, that several years earlier he had supplied racial "pedigrees" on two people to a Washington, D.C. cemetery and that as a result the "burials were stopped in both instances." Further, the cemetery secretary was advised that even though there was no law preventing it and although the burial was in the " 'Pauper Section'...to the white owner of a lot, it might prove embarrassing to meet with negroes visiting at one of their graves on the adjoining lot."

Virginia's race integrity law did, in fact, address only the integrity or "purity" of one race, whites or caucasians. It did not speak at all about marriages between other racial groups and its effect was to create two races "white" and "colored." The best illustration of this effect that I have found was in the way Plecker answered inquires concerning the racial status of certain immigrants. In an October 4, 1935 response to a question about the status of a person from the Philippines he answered:

> In reply to your inquiry as to the racial classification of a native Filipino. I beg to advise that they, as well as Asiatics, including Chinese, Japanese, natives of India, etc., are classed as colored and included with the colored in compiling the statistics.
>
> Under the law of Virginia, Filipinos and other Asiatics are not permitted to marry white people. The child will be classed as colored.

Another case in August, 1940 further illustrates Plecker's convoluted reasoning on race. This case also involved a person of Philippine heritage. It exemplifies as well the fact that the "burden of proof" of racial origins was placed on the individual whose heritage was being questioned, not on the State. The usual mode of operation was that Plecker would make charges concerning race and challenge the implicated person to prove him wrong. To "prove" one's racial heritage is not only difficult, it is ultimately impossible. Those who spoke most stridently of race purity would have been incapable of proving without a doubt the racial integrity of their own ancestors over the centuries. Still, in the name or science and medicine, Plecker continued his hunting for violations of race integrity and the persecution of those he judged to be impure.

> We have your certificate for the marriage, February 28, 1940, of _____, a native of the Philippine Islands, and _____, an Italian born in Pittsburgh, Pennsylvania.
>
> If we are correct in assuming that the woman is white, then under the law of Virginia, you as Clerk [of Courts] were not authorized to issue a marriage license to a person of any of the colored races, including Filipinos. The Racial Integrity Act of 1924...clearly specifies that no marriages can legally occur between a white person and one of any of the colored races, including Malay, to which racial subdivision the Filipinos belong. As it is illegal for this license to have been issued under the laws of Virginia, the marriage itself could not have been legally performed. I am calling your attention to this matter that you may take such action as you deem advisable.
>
> The Italians from the Island of Sicily are badly mixed with former negro slaves, and if this woman is from these, it is barely possible that she herself would have a trace of negro blood and would be eligible for marriage to a Filipino. Proving this would probably be impossible.

Dr. Plecker's confidence as exercised in the making of long distance decisions on racial classification of people seems to have extended to mental disability decisions as well. The superintendent of a county welfare board wrote to him on July 27, 1943 describing a situation she had encountered and asking for his advice. She said that the promiscuous sexual habits of a woman whom she characterized as being feebleminded had led to the birth of two illegitimate children. She suspected that the children were of mixed race but was uncertain of how to make a definite determination of their race. She was also seeking consultation on the best course of action with the woman in the future. Plecker's advice was characteristically simple and direct on both matters. His answer to the question of race in this case again illustrates the questionable nature of the whole race purity campaign and his advice for the woman's future, made with no diagnostic information other than that she had been called feebleminded, is chilling.

> ...As to deciding the point of race, you and the sheriff, and any other intelligent citizen of your community, are as capable of judging from the appearance of the child as the most learned scientist. There is absolutely no blood or other test to determine that question—only the appearance of the children and the habits of the mother as to association with negroes.

> The proper thing to do without loss of time is to place this woman in the State Colony and have her sterilized.

Walter Plecker was fifty-one years old when he became the first State Registrar of Vital Statistics. When he resigned the post in 1946 he was eighty-five. For thirty-four years he had directed the recording and maintenance of information concerning births, deaths, marriages, and other facts about the lives of the people of the Commonwealth of Virginia. More importantly, however, he had intervened directly in the most personal and valued areas of the lives of thousands. He had literally had a voice in births, marriages, and deaths of these people. He had dictated to many of them the race by which they would be recognized regardless of the identity they held of themselves. Dr. Plecker had also influenced attitudes, laws, and practices relating to race at the state, national and international levels. It is curious that a person whose primary responsibility was the collecting and maintenance of information should have been so involved in such matters. It appears, however, that Walter Plecker had the freedom to define his own agenda and that primary on that agenda was the cause of race integrity. In his letter of resignation on May 27, 1946 he made his priorities very clear:

> I am laying down this, my chief life work, with mingled feeling[s] of pleasure and regret—regret at relinquishing this branch of health work, in which I have been greatly interested—pleasure in knowing that I will thus find time to pursue further some ethnological studies in which I am interested.
>
> In this work I will find need for reference to the valuable racial files which have been for years accumulating in Miss Kelley's office [Miss Kelley was his chief "racial" assistant], and which are unequaled for an entire State population anywhere in this or other countries.
>
> I would be glad also for a while to assist Miss Kelley in the great struggle in which she is involved in preserving correct registration of this population as to racial composition, and as a result therefrom the prevention of illegal racial intermarriage and speedier amalgamation. I can be of assistance to her by assuming the responsibility of conducting with her the correspondence involved...
>
> A plan that occurs to me is to be appointed by the Health Department or yourself to a new position—'Ethnologist'—without salary, or at a nominal one of one dollar a year. That will allow me to render Miss Kelley aid in an official capacity...

On his final day on the job Dr. Plecker wrote to his friend John Powell informing him of his resignation. He also reminded Powell that since he was resigning that the copies of letters relating to racial matters that Powell had been receiving for years would no longer be coming to him. Incredibly, he admitted that some of the letters he had sent charging race mixing had been inaccurate! He left it to Powell's discretion as to whether to keep the racially related correspondence or destroy it. Obviously John Powell chose to keep the letters. Of course I'm glad that he did, otherwise I could not have told this part of the tragic but important story with which we are now engaged:

Dear Mr. Powell:

With today my service as State Registrar of Vital Statistics ends. I am now past 85 years of age and have resigned for that reason...With this bunch of letters, your receipt of such copies will likewise end. If you have preserved them, you have a pretty good history of the various racial problems which have come before us since we began sending you these. Copies of all of the letters relating to that subject have been sent you. In some cases no mixture was found. Such letters, if possible, should be eliminated. As I do not know who my successor will be and whether he is at all interested in that subject and this correspondence may ultimately be destroyed or lost, your copies would furnish a pretty good outline of the situation. If, however, you think it is not worth the trouble to preserve them, act upon your judgement and either keep or destroy them.

References

Plecker, Walter, (1924), April 30 letter to Lynchburg woman, John Powell Collection, Alderman Library, University of Virginia.

_____, (1924), April 30 letter to midwife, John Powell Collection, Alderman Library, University of Virginia.

_____, (1924), July 31 letter to R. N. Anderson, John Powell Collection, Alderman Library, University of Virginia.

_____, (1925), March 13 letter to Editor, *Survey Graphic*, John Powell Collection, Alderman Library, University of Virginia.

_____, (1925), May 21 letter to John Gailey, John Powell Collection, Alderman Library, University of Virginia.

_____, (1935), October 4 letter to Grace Davidson, John Powell Collection, Alderman Library, University of Virginia.

_____, (1940), July 11 letter to Dr. H. V. Fitzgerald, John Powell Collection, Alderman Library, University of Virginia.

_____, (1940), August 1 letter to Superintendent, John Powell Collection, Alderman Library, University of Virginia.

_____, (1940), August 3 letter to W. G. Muncy, John Powell Collection, Alderman Library, University of Virginia.

_____, (1940), August 21 letter to A. H. Crismond, John Powell Collection, Alderman Library, University of Virginia.

_____, (1940), September 6 letter to Horace Sutherland, John Powell Collection, Alderman Library, University of Virginia.

_____, (1943), July 27 letter to Nancy Hundley, John Powell Collection, Alderman Library, University of Virginia.

_____, (1946), May 27 letter to J. C. Riggins, John Powell Collection, Alderman Library, University of Virginia.

_____, (1946), June 29 letter to John Powell, John Powell Collection, Alderman Library, University of Virginia.

_____, (no date), "Description of Duties," John Powell Collection, Alderman Library, University of Virginia.

"Racial Integrity...," (1924), *Virginia Pilot and Norfolk Landmark*, February 19, p. 4.

CHAPTER SIX:

Dr. Plecker's War on the Indians

The first two legal challenges to the 1924 racial integrity legislation occurred in the same courtroom before Circuit Court Judge Henry Holt. Both challenges arose from complaints against the Clerk of Rockbridge County. In the first case the Clerk refused to issue a marriage license to a woman named Dorothy Johns. His refusal was based on his conviction that Dorothy was of racially mixed heritage and that he could not, according to the new law, issue her a license to marry a white man. She brought a mandamus action against the Clerk to compel him to issue the license. Witnesses for Dorothy Johns testified that she and her ancestors did not have any mixture of negro blood. Dr. Plecker testified as an expert witness and produced old records which showed that some of Dorothy John's ancestors had been recorded as "colored." Her attorney argued that "colored" in the context of the old records that Plecker was referring to meant "Indian;" that the term had been used to designate white/Indian mixtures. He then produced supporting testimony that Dorothy Johns did, in fact, have Indian ancestors. Another witness testified, however, that he had known the family for several generations and that they were definitely of mixed black ancestry.

In his decision Judge Holt ruled in favor of the Clerk and sustained his refusal to issue the marriage license. While he found in this case that there was convincing evidence for black/white racial mixture, he raised an objection to the racial integrity law itself. He argued that people who might be charged inaccurately with having a racially impure background would find it very difficult to produce documentary evidence to disprove such charges. Judge Holt would later have the opportunity to return to and elaborate upon this concern.

The second challenge to the law came from a relative of Dorothy Johns; her name was Atha Sorrels. Again the Clerk of Rockbridge County refused to issue a marriage license; this time to a man who wanted to marry Atha Sorrels. He invoked the 1924 law, claimed that the man was white, that the woman he wished to marry was not of "pure white race" and refused them a license. The attorney for Atha Sorrels introduced testimony that her family history did not include "negro blood" and that the term "colored" in reference to her family in some records was actually, as had been argued in the Dorothy Johns case, an allusion to Indian blood. Unlike the case of Dorothy Johns, no witness appeared to testify that Atha Sorrels had a black race mixture in her genealogy. Judge Holt decided in favor of Atha Sorrels. He declared that there was no evidence that she was of mixed heritage according to the parameters of the law and that a license should be issued to Atha Sorrels and the man who wished to marry her.

Holt rendered his decision in November of 1924. His decision is important not only for the fact that it gave credence to this challenge to the racial integrity law which had only been enacted earlier that year. It is also important because of Judge Holt's observations on the law and its questionable tests of racial purity.

> I am in cordial sympathy with the general purpose of the statute. Whether it be based upon pride, prejudice or instinct, we look upon ourselves as a sceptered race and stand for its preservation in all its integrity. This purpose has been frequently expressed in our statute law, and miscegenation has always been a felony in this State, but the statute in judgment goes far beyond anything that has heretofore been enacted. It provides that when the Clerk has reason to believe the applicant is not of pure white race, he shall withhold the granting of a marriage to him and to a white person. It further provides that no license shall be granted where there is any *'trace whatsoever'* of alien blood. And that 'the term white person shall apply only to persons who have *no trace whatsoever* of any blood other than Caucasian' excepting those who have one sixteenth or less blood of American Indians.
>
> The Clerk in refusing license is not required to take evidence and can act without a hearing. Of course, if the statute stopped here, we would have want of due process of law.
>
> What further relief is possible? An indirect appeal by way of mandamus to the Clerk may be had to the Court, the burden of proof being upon the applicant. If we apply the statute literally, the relief granted is no relief at all. In twenty-five generations one has thirty-two millions of grandfathers, not to speak of grandmothers, assuming there is no intermarriage [among these ancestors]. Half the men who fought at Hastings were my grandfathers. Some of them were probably hanged and some knighted. Who can tell? Certainly in some instances there was an alien strain. Beyond peradventure I cannot prove that there was not, and so the relief granted by appeal is no relief at all, nor would the results be different if we were to treat the Clerk as a court with power to enter final judgement.
>
> There is no inhibition against the intermarriage of those who are unable to prove absence of a trace of blood of stock prohibited, and since, nobody can prove this, we find ourselves where we were in the beginning. Alice herself never got into a deeper tangle.

Judge Holt continued through his decision to criticize the race integrity statute for the poorly defined racial concepts it contained. He pointed out, for example, that the law defined white people as being those who are of "pure Caucasian blood." He consulted several sources and could not find two authorities who agreed on the meaning of the term and came to the conclusion that in the field of ethnology at that time Caucasian had no definite meaning.

Because of this lack of meaning of the very term Caucasian and the impossibility of tracing and proving one's "racial purity" back through countless generations, Holt held that reason and judgement, rather than points of law, must prevail in Atha Sorrels' case. He closed his decision with the following remarks:

> If we discard the letter of the law and apply as we must, if it is to stand at all, the 'rule of reason' which is that there must be present an appreciable amount of foreign [non-white] blood, I am of opinion that the evidence in this case which covers a period of 130 years, certainly the weight of it is to the effect that there is no strain present in the applicant of any blood other than white, except Indian, and there is not enough of that to come within the statute. The license should issue.

The decision in the Sorrels case was most disturbing to John Powell, Walter Plecker and their colleagues in the Anglo-Saxon Clubs. Powell authored a pamphlet critical of the circumstances and the decision in the case. The pamphlet entitled, *The Breach in the Dyke: An Analysis of the Sorrels Case Showing the Danger to Racial Integrity from Intermarriage of Whites with So-Called Indians*, was published and distributed by the Anglo-Saxon Clubs. A typed manuscript in the Powell Collection appears to be a rough draft of that pamphlet. It is entitled in handwriting "The Sorrels Case" with authorship indicated as John Powell. For whatever personal and political reasons, in this piece Powell was uncharacteristically gentle and polite with someone who disagreed with him on a racial issue. He spoke with understanding of Judge Holt's decision in the Sorrels case. As we shall see, it may have been that Powell understood that Henry Holt agreed with him on racial issues but was compelled to make the decision he made by the circumstances of the presentation of the case. John Powell gives his impressions of the trial:

> ...Superficially regarded, the evidence, if accepted uncritically, could justify no other decision than that rendered by Judge Holt, namely, that Atha Sorrels was not negroid, and that the license should issue.
>
> Now I was present at that trial. I went there with an open mind...I freely admit that apart from the evidence of Dr. Plecker and his records, the defense [of the clerk who refused to issue the license] introduced no testimony upon which a case could be based. And yet, I left the court convinced of the propriety of the clerk's refusal to issue [the] license... The case is so typical and can have such colossal bearing upon the future of our people, that it will well repay us to examine the evidence in some detail...
>
> Early in the course of the proceedings...chief counsel for Atha Sorrels, introduced a blue-print, alleged to be the family tree of the complainant...The purpose of this print seemed to be the establishment of the Indian descent of Atha Sorrels. Among the ancestors thereon inscribed was one James Clark, who in 1876 had been declared white by the court, after bringing mandamus action to compel the clerk to grant him license to marry a white woman...In it James Clark claimed to be 'less than one-fourth negro or Indian.' [Atha Sorrels' attorney] claimed that the success of...Clark's action had established...the right of him and his descendants to the status of whites; that the phrase in the petition 'less than one-fourth negro' was not to be taken literally,

but was purely technical, and that the addition of the words, 'or Indian' should
be taken as proof that there was no other non-Caucasic strain than Indian...
...Dr. Plecker introduced state records showing that Clark ancestors of
Atha Sorrels were entered as 'free colored.' [Atha Sorrels' attorney] claimed
that 'free colored' did not necessarily mean negro; that the Clark's were of
Indian descent, and as there was no column for Indians in the [state] forms
they had been put...in the colored column.

Powell also gives an account of Dr. Plecker's further arguments and the
testimony of other witnesses. None of them, however, were able to give
convincing evidence that Atha Sorrels was of mixed black descent. Powell
states rather straight forwardly that Judge Holt found that the weight of the
evidence was that she had no mixture of blood other than Indian and that the
marriage license should be issued. He then makes an interesting comment
about Judge Holt's remarks supporting his decision:

[Judge Holt] then stated verbally that he would like to see the case
appealed. Had the Judge been content with this, the matter would not be very
serious. However, the major portion of his opinion was taken up with an attack
on the Racial Integrity law. His grounds for criticism were not the same as
those expressed in his [Dorothy] Johns case decision. In his Sorrels decision he
states that the law is so vague as to be impossible of literal application. He
claims that if we were to go back twenty-five generations not one of us could
prove that among our thirty-two million ancestors there was not one of
non-white blood. The implication is that a fanatical or malicious clerk could
make it impossible for any one in Virginia to obtain a marriage license. In
answer to this let me point out that under the law the clerk must have a 'reasonable' doubt of the racial purity of the applicant before he may withhold the
license. It seems scarcely probable that any court would recognize as 'reasonable' a doubt based upon the possibility that one of the thirty-two million
ancestors, living a thousand years ago may have been colored.

Judge Holt also objects to the use of the word 'Caucasian,' stating that
authorities disagree as to its meaning...

I cannot but feel that Judge Holt has been too meticulous in his
objections to the law. However, if his decision is allowed to stand, it will mean
the complete nullification of our most precious possession, our race records,
[those of] 1853–1896, our greatest protection against the infusion of negro
blood. If this decision is to stand, any negroid in the state can go before a court
and say, 'My ancestors are recorded as colored, but that does not mean negro,
they were Indians.' He may then be declared white and may marry a white
woman. Many negroes are already attempting to claim the status of Indians, as
Dr. Plecker pointed out. Indians are springing up all over the state as if by
spontaneous generation. We cannot suffer this outrage to continue. If we are
to preserve our civilization, our ideals, the soul of our race, we must call a
halt...The Sorrels case must be appealed!

Powell's demand for an appeal, however, would be withdrawn. After
consultation with the Office of the Attorney General of Virginia he decided
that an appeal would be too risky. He was advised that there was a risk that the
Racial Integrity Act could be declared unconstitutional under the scrutiny of

an appeal. A letter from Assistant Attorney General Leon Bazile on November 26, 1924 made the risk very evident:

My dear Mr. Powell:

I have heard from the Commonwealth's Attorney of Rockbridge County with reference to the Sorrells case, and he informs us that in the event that the State should appeal, Judge Holt says he will amend his opinion, and declare the racial integrity act unconstitutional.

Of course, if you and Dr. Plecker wish the case to go to the Court of Appeals, this office will take it there, but the thought has occurred to me that inasmuch as the law seems to be working all right outside of Judge Holt's circuit, we would run the risk of losing a great deal on the chance of reversing him in one case. I would be very glad if you would write me your views about this matter, as something has to be done about appealing this case within the next few days.

On April 6, 1925 John Powell wrote to Judge Holt explaining that he had decided, on behalf of the Anglo-Saxon Clubs, not to appeal the Sorrels case saying that it was "too dubious to justify the risk." He also sent Holt a copy of his pamphlet, *The Breach in the Dyke*, and invited his comments. Once again he was seemingly most gracious to Holt: "so anxious am I to preserve the amenities and proprieties, that I am unwilling to proceed with the matter until you yourself have been given the opportunity to express your feelings." Surely this graciousness did not compensate, however, for Powell's charges in the pamphlet that Judge Holt was attacking the racial integrity law and that his meticulous objections to the law were threatening the purity of the white race in Virginia. Judge Holt's response three days later to Powell's letter and pamphlet was cool and reasoned.

My dear Mr. Powell:

I thank you for your article on racial integrity which reached me this morning. So far as I am advised, there is no white man in Virginia who does not wish to see it preserved. The difficulties presented in the statute can be so readily met by amendments that a failure to do this would indicate interest in the shadow rather than the substance.

My views in the Atha Sorrels case are in writing. I have no pride of opinion and have done what I could to make an appeal in that case easy. The Supreme Court of Appeals of Virginia is the tribunal before which criticism can best be presented. That dispassionate court will not hesitate to reverse my judgement should it be of opinion that it is erroneous, should it be affirmed that affirmation would be a complete answer to the criticisms to which I have been subjected. The question is one of law and presents as little field for feeling as does the multiplication table.

The risk that Henry Holt's judgment would be 'affirmed' in this way was never taken, the law was never tested by an appeal of the Sorrels case. The real importance of the case was that it portrayed the impossibility of producing proof of racial heritage as called for by the law. It showed that placing the burden of proof on the individual whose race was being questioned was an unreasonable requirement. Equally important, the case demonstrated that the records that Dr. Plecker had produced as evidence of the racial background of Atha Sorrels and her relatives were not convincing as legal proof that they had black ancestry.

Given the judgement on the validity of these records, and the fear that an appeal would prove to be unsuccessful, it is amazing how boldly the march for race purity by Powell, Plecker and their colleagues continued. This is particularly true of Walter Plecker's campaign against people claiming native American heritage.

In fact the weaknesses in the law and in the kind of evidence being used in its execution was further demonstrated in another case in 1925. This case is discussed by Brian Thomson in his 1978 dissertation on Virginia's race integrity legislation. Ray Winn was a member of the Chickahominy Indian group. He and his first wife were married as Indians in New Kent County. After his first wife died, he married May Wilson, a white woman. He was subsequently indicted on the charge that as a "colored" man he had intermarried with a white woman. The case was heard in the Hustings Court in Richmond. In court the same sort of records which had been presented in the Sorrels case were introduced to prove that Ray Winn had black ancestors. Numerous witnesses, however, testified that they had known his family for generations and that they were Indians and whites. The decision of the Hustings Court on December 11, 1925, was that the evidence did not sustain the charge. This judgement, of course, cast even further discredit on the records that Walter Plecker believed were conclusive evidence of the race of so many people in Virginia.

Walter Plecker's battle against those people who identified themselves as being of Native American heritage was broad and vigorous. He was obsessed with the idea that literally all those people who claimed to be of Indian descent in Virginia were perpetuating a falsehood. He was compulsive in collecting information which he thought added proof to this argument. He also identified some individuals and certain families as special subjects of his campaign, and he pursued them with a vengeance.

A letter from Plecker to a man named D. E. Harrower on April 27, 1925 helps to make clear his thoughts and passion on the question of Indians in Virginia. I have come to believe that although Plecker was initially irritated by what he saw as the use of the claim of "Indian" as a loophole in the race integrity law, he came to resent the concept that there was any existing vestige of the Native American race in Virginia. In his letter to Harrower, who had apparently written earlier with opinions supporting the legitimacy of Indian claims in Virginia, Plecker leaves no room for them at all as a valid racial group.

> As you doubtless know, my responsibility in the matter arises under the new 'Racial Integrity' law, due to the fact that as State Registrar of births, deaths, marriages and divorces it becomes my duty to register these events correctly as to color, under that law.

That act of 1925 defines a white person as one 'who has no trace whatsoever of any blood other than Caucasian, but persons who have one-sixteenth or less of the blood of the American Indian and have no other non-Caucasic blood shall be deemed to be white persons.'

For any person, therefore, to claim to be an Indian so as to be eligible for inter-marriage with whites, it is necessary for him to show that there has never been any introduction of negro blood into his family.

Plecker followed these comments with a litany of indictments against the various groups in Virginia who claimed to be Indians. His list was encompassing and accusing.

...there are probably no native Virginia Indians unmixed with negro.

Our office is in possession of old birth, death and marriage records reaching back to 1853. The marriages were reported by the county clerks to the State Auditor at the end of each year, and indicated whether the parties were white or 'Free Negroes' (prior to 1865)...These old records are now in our keeping. In practically every case where the pedigree of these so-called 'Indians' has been investigated it has been found to be founded upon this free negro blood.

These freed negroes, usually the off-spring by male members of their master's families and negro women, considered themselves superior to the slave negro, and intermarried amongst themselves and with any remnants of Indians which may still have existed, thus accounting for their claim to being 'Indians.' As a slight admixture of Indian blood seems to show plainly in many cases, they have been able, by keeping up for several generations their shout that 'we are Indians,' to have induced many, who should know better, to lazily admit it, regardless of the fact that negro blood was really the predominating colored admixture.

Plecker then proceeded in his letter to discount the claims to Indian heritage of each Native American group in Virginia. The Pamunkeys he discounted as "heavily mixed with negro and white"...[with] "a faint trace of Indian." He described the Rappahannocks as a "group of similar origin [that] have about the same claim to being Indians." Of the Indian group of which Atha Sorrels and Dorothy Johns were a part he said, "The Amherst-Rockbridge group of about 800 similar people, are giving us the most trouble, through actual numbers and persistent claims of being Indians." Plecker claimed of the Chickahominy Indians that "their existence as a tribe was a political trick, to enable the white people to maintain control of the county government, Indians not being voters."

Plecker closed his letter to Mr. Harrower with a proclamation and a challenge. "As it is my task to warn the people of Virginia against intermarriage with persons of negro descent, I expect to continue my warning until you...and others, produce more satisfactory proof than has been brought out, that these people are entirely free from negro mixture."

While doing research at the American Philosophical Society Library in Philadelphia I came across an exchange of correspondence that sheds a different and interesting light on Walter Plecker's Indian campaign. The letters were written by Plecker and by a man who used both the name Reverend Doctor R. F. St. James and the Indian name Shiuhushu. Reverend St. James' correspondence was written on letterhead of the American Indian Association in Denver, Colorado. The nature of the dialogue between Plecker and St. James is very reminiscent of the alliance between Marcus Garvey's Universal Negro Improvement Association, and John Powell, Walter Plecker and the Anglo-Saxon Clubs. The "strange bedfellows" cliche immediately comes to mind when reading the exchange between an Indian leader, at least a self-proclaimed leader, and the man who devoted two decades to the proposition that Native Americans did not exist as a race in Virginia. Plecker may have used some combination of intimidation and flattery with St. James in earlier letters. From the later letters it is obvious that St. James was on the defensive about his own racial purity and that of the Indian group in the Western United States that he represented. In defense of his own people perhaps, he was willing to join Plecker in his criticism of other groups claiming Indian heritage. In an August 25, 1926 letter from St. James to Plecker (also dated "Thunder Moon, 26 Suns, 1926 Great Suns") the Indian leader said:

> Yes, we do very firmly stand on that one question, we consider it serious, and, of great importance both for the welfare of the Red and White Races. We are the only Indian Organization, boldly comes out strongly, bar out from membership any person with Negro Blood.
> The Negro has his place, and should be made to understand to keep it...
> We have a Negro problem on hand, we all must fight, and fight hard, and stir up pride in this respect. They are other Indian Organizations, both in East and West, we know have in their membership Negro blood, and these organizations are somewhat sore at us, the stand we take, and these with both Indian and negro mixture are the ones causes trouble, because we oppose them, we will not stand for it.

Attached to this letter was also an official statement from the American Indian Association. It appears to have been an attempt to placate Plecker and to put distance between itself and the subjects of his witch hunt. The statement was signed by St. James, by Chief Joseph Strong Wolfe, and by the organization's General National Secretary, Flying Eagle Stagg.

> To Whom It May Concern:
> The American Indian Association, and American Indian Order, Including our Ladies Councils of the Daughters of [S]acajawea, that all persons, if it be Indian, or white, with negro blood, we consider them as negro. And should be classified as negro, no matter what part of the United States they are.
> The Indians in the State of Virginia that are mix with any percentage of negro blood should not be classified as Indians, but classified these Indians-mix-negro as negro, and should be subject to Jim Crow law of the South. Indians that are real Indians should show evidence on trains that he or she is Indian and not negro. Again no person with negro blood can be entitled to membership of our organization.

Dr. Plecker was obviously very pleased to have this organization as an ally in his cause. On September 1 he replied, "I have your letter of August 26th together with the certificate of the decision of the American Indian Association, Inc., as to the racial standing of our Virginia mixed breeds. I am glad to have your association come out this positively on the subject." Even the concessionary nature of the association's statement was not enough, however, to completely satisfy Plecker. He found a point on which to correct and instruct St. James.

> You speak of 'pure Indians of Virginia and Indians of white blood only.' I want to make it plain that such do not exist. The authorities that I have called your attention to and our own observation point clearly to the fact that there are no pure Indians unmixed with negro in the State, except three or four who came here, one from Oklahoma and the others from Texas, who are probably unmixed with any except white blood. They married into white families and have remained in Virginia. Those are entitled to be classed as Indians—no others.

> I am glad to know that you are considering a visit to Virginia and hope to address various gatherings of people. When you come we hope to have a visit from you in our office in the State Office Building, Capitol Square, but be sure before you recognize any groups as Indian and white without negro mixture that you give it very careful consideration. Should you admit any of these, the thinking white people will immediately put you in the same class with them.

Dr. Plecker maintained correspondence with Charles Davenport, the director of the Eugenics Record Office. Davenport was one of the deans of the American eugenics movement. Included in his own research was a study race mixing in Jamaica. Some of the other work supported by his office also touched on race issues and the study of one Indian group by A. H. Estabrook, a researcher from the Eugenics Record Office, was of major interest to Plecker. Letters in the Davenport Collection at the American Philosophical Society Library show that Plecker and Davenport corresponded a great deal about the Shinecock Indians of New York. At one time Davenport mistakenly reported to Plecker that the state legislature had abolished reservations for the Shinecock because there were no "pure" Indians left in the group. Although this report was eventually proved to be incorrect, when first told of it Plecker was excited and planned to use the information in his own Indian "battle."

Plecker wrote to Davenport with news of his correspondence with R. F. St. James of the American Indian Association, and sent him a copy of the organization's proclamation. His comments to Davenport provide a bit more background:

> I received recently a rather discourteous letter from R. F. St. James, then at Denver, Colorado, who seems to represent the American Indian Association. He was indignant over a report made to him that I had referred...to all Indians as being negroid. Of course, that is without any foundation. In my reply I called upon him to apologize for his rudeness and then discussed at some length the situation in Virginia, calling upon him to cooperate in our effort to properly classify our Virginia mixed breeds.

> I am sending you a copy of his letter of August 26th, together with a proclamation from the Association in reference to our Virginia 'Indians'...I

believe that if we can tie him up with our move to properly list our Virginia mixed breeds that it will be of material assistance...

I have already had some correspondence with the U.S. Bureau of Census in reference to properly classifying them at the next Census. They asked me to take the matter up with them in 1929.

In another letter to Davenport on September 9, 1926, Plecker makes a statement which demonstrates that his encouragement of the Indian leader was only manipulative. It also illustrates the deep disregard that Plecker had for anyone identifying themselves as Indian. "I received another letter from Rev. Red Fox St. James, of the American Indian Association, who seems to be very zealous about protecting the Indian race against intermixture with negroes. I think, however, that they [the Indians] are eager to lose themselves in the white race."

For years and in many different contexts Plecker repeated his denial that Indians were a legitimate racial group in Virginia. He continued his charges also that these groups were actually "mulattoes" trying to secure recognition as Indians as a step toward admittance into the white race. He voiced these positions to politicians, to bureaucrats, to academicians, and to anyone else of influence he could reach. He was infuriated when anthropologists or historians argued on behalf of the existence of legitimate Indian groups in the state. In many cases related to questions of Indian heritage he literally took the law into his own hands. He made decisions that were clearly not his to make.

On April 17, 1940 he wrote to the President of Radford State Teachers College advising him on an admission question:

We have your letter of April 15, asking whether Indians (Cherokees of North Carolina) are barred from enrolling in State institutions of higher learning of Virginia by reason of race...[The] law has been generally interpreted by school authorities to prevent the admittance of any colored races into the white schools, though that point is not specially referred to in the racial integrity act. The general purpose is to forbid the intermixture in State schools of young persons when it is not legal for them to intermarry. Since the law forbids the marriage of a Cherokee Indian and a white person in Virginia, my own interpretation of the matter would be that the admission of any of the colored races into a white school is not permissible. However, the Attorney General has not as far as I know ruled upon the question.

You are doubtless familiar with the fact that in past years western Indians were admitted into the Normal and Agricultural Institute (negro) at Hampton, Virginia., I have myself seen individuals among them who could easily pass as white...I know of no cases in which the State white schools have admitted Indians. I believe it would be safer to avoid establishing a precedent.

In hundreds of cases Walter Plecker refused to process birth or marriage certificates with racial designations which he felt were incorrect. His judgments were often based only on a family name and the county where the certificate had been filed. As mentioned earlier, he maintained lists of names and often acted on the basis of these names and no other evidence. His refusal to issue certificates on this basis was clearly improper and was eventually proven to be illegal. It must also have been terribly hurtful and demeaning to those families that were repeatedly abused in this fashion. In most of these instances, however, there is no evidence of an appeal of any sort. Dr. Walter Plecker was the absolute authority in these matters and his power was largely uncontested. A letter written on July 13, 1940 by Plecker is an example of how he, on the basis of supposition, dictated to an individual how his race was to be officially designated.

> We are returning the certificate in duplicate for your birth of June 15, 1906. Under this form of registration we account only such certificates as reach us in a satisfactory manner and that we believe to be accurate.
>
> In giving your race you state that you are a 'Black Hark Indian' and that your birthplace was Delaware Water Gap. We have learned that none of the native-born individuals in Virginia claiming to be Indian are free from negro mixture,and under the law of Virginia every person with any ascertainable degree of negro blood is to be classed as a negro or colored person, not as an Indian. In Delaware there is a similar group locally known as 'Moors,' who, like our Virginia mulattoes, are claiming to be pure Indian, unmixed with negro. They may be able to get by with that in Delaware, but we do not accept such classification in Virginia.
>
> If you desire to make out a new certificate...in which you give your race as colored or negro, the certificate will otherwise be acceptable. The fact that your wife is negro would seem to show conclusively that that is the correct classification.

Perhaps the best way to close this chapter is with a quote that may illustrate Walter Plecker's single minded commitment to his crusade and his obliviousness to the wider implications of what he was doing. In a letter to the Commissioner of Indian Affairs in April of 1943, Plecker answered a complaint which had been lodged with the Commissioner's Office by a woman who claimed Indian status on the birth certificate of her child. She complained that her designation had not been honored and that she had been harassed. Apparently a person on the Commissioner's staff had advised him of Plecker's "lists" and drawn a parallel with the Nazi "race hygiene" program. Plecker acknowledged the comparison with seeming pride.

> We would be delighted to have you or your representative visit our office and examine the mass of original information and pedigree charts...showing the racial origin of mixed breeds trying to pass as Indian or white. Our own indexed birth and marriage records, showing race, reach back to 1853. Such a study has probably never been made before. Your staff member is probably correct in his surmise that Hitler's genealogical study of the Jews is not more complete.

References

Bazile, Leon, (1924), November 26 letter to John Powell, John Powell Collection, Alderman Library, University of Virginia.

Holt, Henry W., (1924), Decision in Atha Sorrels v. A. T. Shields, Clerk, 18th Judicial Circuit Court, Staunton, Virginia.

_____, (1925), April 9 letter to John Powell, John Powell Collection, Alderman Library, University of Virginia.

Plecker, Walter, (1925), April 6 letter to Judge Henry Holt, John Powell Collection, Alderman Library, University of Virginia.

_____, (1925), April 27 letter to D. E. Harrower, John Powell Collection, Alderman Library, University of Virginia.

_____, (1926), September 1 letter to R. F. St. James, Charles Davenport Collection, American Philosophical Society Library, Philadelphia.

_____, (1926), September 1 letter to Charles Davenport, Charles Davenport Collection, American Philosophical Society Library, Philadelphia.

_____, (1926), September 9 letter to Charles Davenport, Charles Davenport Collection, American Philosophical Society Library, Philadelphia.

_____, (1940), April 17 letter to Dr. David Peters, John Powell Collection, Alderman Library, University of Virginia

_____, (1940), July 13 letter, John Powell Collection, Alderman Library, University of Virginia.

_____, (1943), April 6 letter to Commissioner John Collier, John Powell Collection, Alderman Library, University of Virginia.

Powell, John, (no date), "The Sorrels Case," John Powell Collection, Alderman Library, University of Virginia.

St. James, R. F., (1926), August 26 letter to W. A. Plecker.

Charles Davenport Collection, American Philosophical Society Library, Philadelphia.

Thomson, Brian W., (1978), *Racism and Racial Classification: A Case Study of the Virginia Racial Integrity Legislation*, Dissertation: University of California at Riverside.

CHAPTER SEVEN:

Human Beings as Mongrels, A Eugenic Tragedy

Arthur Estabrook was involved as a eugenic expert in the sterilization trial of Carrie Buck. He was given the assignment of substantiating her defective hereditary makeup through field research in the area where she grew up and went to school. The information and the witnesses he gathered as an expert assigned by the Eugenics Record Office were crucial to the case. In fact, however, Estabrook came to Virginia earlier on another mission. He had come originally to Amherst County to study a group of Indian people there who had caught his interest.

Eugenicists had long been interested in the assumed negative effects of "race mixing." The Amherst Indian group was claimed by Estabrook, along with Plecker, to be tri-racial, a mix of Indian, white, and black people. This, of course, would be a tempting subject for a eugenic researcher of Estabrook's ilk. As early as February 10, 1923 he wrote to Charles Davenport, Director of the Eugenic Record Office, reporting that he had begun to collect data on the group. On March 5 of that year Davenport wrote expressing approval of Estabrook's involvement in the Amherst research project.

Dear Dr. Estabrook:

I have just heard from Professor I. E. McDougle, who tells me that he expects to have all the field material ready by the first of May and would like to have you come to Sweet Briar [College] for a few days to study the collected material and either write it up or go after more material. I think this would be a thoroly [sp.] warranted investment of your time. McDougle writes that he has twenty college majors doing field work and he hopes to finish it up in two or three weeks...

Sincerely yours,

The work did seem to progress quickly and efficiently. By August 4 Estabrook included the following comment in a letter to Davenport.

...field work was carried out for a period of a month or so in Amherst County, Virginia where an Indian/negro/white cross was studied in collaboration with the Sociology Department of Sweet Briar College, located near the area. The senior students in this department carried on field work under the immediate direction of Prof. I. E. McDougle of the department and my supervision. Approximately five hundred members of this Amherst group have been located, traced to a common head and studied; much illegitimacy and feeble-mindedness have been found and a low social status present in practically all the huts and log cabins where these folk live. A complete report of the work will be made later...

Indeed a report of the research would be written! An indication of what was to come is contained in Estabrook's annual report for 1923-24 to the Eugenics Record Office.

...The low mental level [of the group] is no doubt due to the preponderance of Indian and negro blood. The data gathered seems to show also that the stolid, unemotional make-up of the Indian and so characteristic of him dominates the light, easy-going, music loving, 'preaching' traits of the negro, for little music is found among these people and no teachers or preachers have been produced from them although there has been [a] school and church [there] for many years.

In 1926, a book with the incredible and disturbing title *Mongrel Virginians* was published. It is the description of the eugenic study of the Amherst Indian group. The title page lists the authors as Arthur H. Estabrook and Ivan E. McDougle, in that order. It is the most blatantly racist of all of the eugenic family pedigree studies. It was hurtful, of course, to the people described in the book who read it. They had cooperated willingly when the researchers came with their questions. Now they felt that their poverty had been misrepresented in the book, and they resented the distortion of their morals and habits it contained. The Indian people of Amherst are still hurting sixty years after the publication of the racist tract. *Mongrel Virginians* was also used in the promotion of racially discriminatory and exclusionary policies by Plecker in Virginia and elsewhere by other race separatists.

Estabrook and McDougle introduced *Mongrel Virginians* by giving a general description of the people. It is a description filled with inaccuracy and bias. It illustrates, however, that from the beginning of the book the Amherst Indians were being used to convey a eugenic lesson. The book uses pseudonyms for place names and people but the location and identities were and are immediately recognizable to anyone familiar with that area of Virginia. So much so in fact that I immediately made the connection when I first discovered a copy of the book several years ago.

Situated in the foothills of the Blue Ridge Mountains in Ab County, Virginia is a group of mixed bloods, known locally by a certain term but designated here as the Win Tribe. [Win being used to designate the claimed mixture of *W*hite, *I*ndian and *N*egro blood.] The general population of Ab County consider them neither white nor negro. The Wins themselves claim to be of Indian descent. They are found in an area approximately eight miles long and varying in width up to four miles. There are about five hundred people in this group. They live generally in log houses or rough shacks; a few are in board houses. They are mostly renters on the land; a few own their own homes and land. Their main source of income is from tobacco...Some few work as laborers for the white farmers near-by. One mission school of a church has furnished practically the only education offered to these folks. This mission also has had a chapel for some twenty years. Transportation into and through the area is easy during the summer months; difficult during the winter...This Win group is set apart because of its 'color' and because it has been considered an inferior set. They take no part in activities outside of their particular area; they have no connection with the political activities in the county in which they live. The white folks look down on them, as do the negroes, and this, with their dark skin color, has caused a segregation from the general community.

They are described variously as 'low down' yellow negroes, as Indians, as 'mixed.' No one, however, speaks of them as white. The Wins themselves in general claim the Indian descent although most of them realize they are 'mixed,' preferring to speak of the 'Indian' rather than of a possibility of a negro mixture in them. A few claim to be white. The term by which they have been known locally for many years is that used to designate the negro slaves who were given their freedom by their masters before the Civil War [Estabrook and McDougle were here referring to the term Issues which was derived from Free Issues. The term has the character of a racial epithet and, unfortunately, is still commonly used]...

The study of this tribe has been carried on from two angles; genetics and from that of sociology. It has been made through search of official records in the Ab County Courthouse and at the Bureau of Vital Statistics of the State of Virginia at Richmond, conferences with white people who have lived in or near the Win region, and the mission workers, past and present, and by visits to the homes of the Wins themselves. The study has included both mental and physical characteristics, modes of living, earning capacity, schooling and special customs. It has lasted over a period of two years beginning in January, 1923. The senior students in sociology in one of the colleges in Virginia [Sweet Briar] have assisted in the field work and in the tabulation of the data gathered.

Most of the rest of the book is a litany of the degeneracy, immorality, irresponsibility and inferiority that Estabrook and McDougle attributed to the Amherst Indian people. Their problems were claimed to be the result of their "mixed blood." *Mongrel Virginians* is largely a morality play cast with the people who had in good faith opened their homes and lives to Estabrook, McDougle and their assistants. Instead of the understanding of their social and economic circumstances that they may have expected from the researchers that they trusted, they were portrayed as mongrels. Estabrook and McDougle argued that because of race mixing:

The whole Win tribe is below the average, mentally and socially. They are lacking in academic ability, industrious to a very limited degree and capable of taking little training...

In their social relationships they represent a very crude type of civilization...life appears to drag along from day to day in the same old dreary way.

The persistency of Indian traits among the Wins appears remarkable...When one sees a group of men walking along the county road they will always be found parading in single file and for the most part noncommunicative. They are all very suspicious but this may be largely due to their geographical and their even greater psychological isolation throughout life. For the most part they are extremely diffident, reserved, timid, graceless, taciturn and very humble...

Unquestionably the people covered by this study represent an ever increasing social problem in the South. Social consciousness [concerning people like them] has only begun to be awakened. Amidst the furor of newspaper and pamphlet publicity on miscegenation which has appeared since the passage of the Virginia Racial Integrity Law of 1924 this study is presented not as theory or as representing a prejudiced point of view but as a careful summary of the facts of history.

The book closes with an appendix which contains the full text of the Virginia Racial Integrity Law of 1924.

From the inclusion of the law in the book and the reference about the authors having consulted records at the Virginia Bureau of Vital Statistics, it might be assumed that Walter Plecker was a party to the research. Plecker's zeal and commitment to eliminating Virginia's Indians may have been too much even for Arthur Estabrook. An interesting set of correspondence in the Charles Davenport Collection in the American Philosophical Society Library in Philadelphia indicates that there was a low level of trust for Plecker within the Eugenic Record Office.

Plecker first wrote to Davenport in late 1924 asking about the status of the Estabrook and McDougle work. A reply indicated to him that the research was not yet ready for publication and that a rewrite of the manuscript using pseudonyms rather than the real names of the people was necessary. Plecker wrote back asking for a copy of the report and permission to copy it. Penciled on the bottom of the letter was a note from Davenport asking Estabrook what he thought of Plecker's request.

A letter from Estabrook to Davenport on January 17, 1925 offers an interesting perspective on Plecker's style and reputation even within the mainline of eugenics.

My dear Dr. Davenport:

Dr. W. A. Plecker's offer to make copies of the Ishy manuscript is due to the fact that he, himself, desires a copy to use, not only in checking his own records, but to use in the various cases now appearing in the Virginia courts where some of the Isshies are filing suits to compel the county clerk to issue either white or Indian registration cards...

Permitting him to have access to these names and data would involve us in a great deal of trouble and I fear publicity that would come back to hurt us. That is my feeling in the matter.

The White America book and the new society started in Richmond 'for the purity of the white race' is egging Dr. Plecker on, and while he says this is only 'Virginia's attempt to settle the race problem,' many people in Virginia feel that he is not attacking the problem correctly.

He has written me several times for the data and I have answered him by saying that I felt nothing should be published until all the field work that was planned had been completed and have put him off that way.

The matter of the data being confidential would not enter into this so much if Dr. Plecker did not wish to use this data in court and further, there would be no assurance on his part that his own copy might not become a public record in his own office.

I would suggest that you write Dr. Plecker that until all the work on the Isshies is completed, that nothing can be made public.

Two days later Davenport wrote to Plecker stating that the information which Estabrook had obtained under the auspices of the Eugenics Record Office had been collected under a pledge of confidentiality. He said that even though the Eugenics Record Office wished to be of use in the "advancement of society," the impression that confidentiality was not honored could impair future research and could not be risked.

Plecker was persistent, however, and in August, 1925 he wrote again asking for the information on the Amherst Indian group. He explained, "I have had a lot of correspondence from the people of the Amherst group clamoring to be registered as white. This group was studied by Estabrook and McDougle. I hope their report will not be long delayed as we need it badly in our work."

In September of the following year Plecker wrote to Estabrook directly seeking the same information. The book had been published and Plecker wanted a key which would allow him to break through the pseudonyms. He also introduced the idea that perhaps Estabrook owed him a favor.

I hope to see you in Richmond sometime. I have been disappointed in not being able to secure from you and Professor McDougle the key to the names of the families referred to in your book 'Mongrel Virginians.' That is a splendid work and would be of inestimable value to our office if we knew the real names of individuals referred to. I have recommended the book to several hundred people and I hope sales have resulted from this recommendation.

Apparently Estabrook evaded Plecker's request and referred him back once again to Davenport. Plecker wrote to Davenport this time as if he had not asked for this information before. Perhaps he had genuinely forgotten his previous requests or it may have simply been the allure of the information which made him persist. Whatever the case, Plecker's final plea for the names of the "Mongrel Virginians" was a strong one. On December 21, 1926 he wrote to Davenport:

The point that I am writing to you about is for your permission for McDougle and Estabrook to furnish us the key to the book, 'Mongrel Virginians,' for use in our office. You know, of course, that it is our problem to decide finally as to the racial status of the people of the State for the purpose of marriage and for their birth records. The charts contained in this book would be of inestimable value to us if we have the key as to the family names.

Dr. Estabrook checked up much of his work in our office and found that our old birth records covering the period from 1853 through 1896 agreed quite closely with the results of his findings and that where they classified these people as mixed our old records show that they were listed as colored during that period.

It would be a great pity for such valuable piece of work not to be made available and to eventually lose its importance as it will, unless it is known as to the families to which reference is made.

Dr. Estabrook says that he expects to see you in a few days and will talk the matter over with you at that time.

Handwritten in the margin of the letter was Davenport's response, "No!" His official response to Plecker was written a few days later. He again explained that confidentiality prevented him from releasing the information to Plecker.

References

Davenport, C., (1923), March 5 letter to A. H. Estabrook, Charles Davenport Collection, American Philosophical Society Library, Philadelphia, PA.

Estabrook, A. H., (1923), August 4 letter to C. Davenport, Charles Davenport Collection, American Philosophical Society Library, Philadelphia, PA.

_____, (1924), *Annual Report for 1923–24 to the Eugenics Record Office*, Charles Davenport Collection, American Philosophical Society Library, Philadelphia, PA.

_____, (1925), January 17 letter to Charles Davenport, Charles Davenport Collection, American Philosophical Society Library, Philadelphia, Pennsylvania.

Estabrook, Arthur H. and McDougle, Ivan E, (1926), *Mongrel Virginians: The Win Tribe*, Baltimore: The Williams and Wilkins Company.

Plecker, Walter A., (1925), August 17 letter to Charles Davenport, Charles Davenport Collection, American Philosophical Society Library, Philadelphia, Pennsylvania.

_____, (1926), September 9 letter to Arthur Estabrook, American Philosophical Society Library, Philadelphia, Pennsylvania.

_____, (1926), December 21 letter to Charles Davenport, Charles Davenport Collection, American Philosophical Society Library, Philadelphia, Pennsylvania.

CHAPTER EIGHT:

Documentary Genocide and The Indians of Amherst

My friend, Dr. Peter Houck, a Lynchburg physician and the author of *Indian Island*, provided me with a copy of a letter which was written by Walter Plecker in December, 1943. The letter was addressed to registrars, court clerks and legislators throughout the state. A few statements from the letter will illustrate that the intensity of Plecker's crusade against Virginia's Indians had not diminished. While reading these statements I found it difficult to believe that these were the words of a state official contained in what was intended to be formal and official correspondence:

> In our January 1943 annual letter to local registrars and clerks of courts, with list of mixed surnames, we called attention to the greatly increased effort and arrogant demands now being made for classification as whites, or at least for recognition as Indians, as a preliminary step to admission into the white race by marriage, of groups of the descendants of the 'free negroes,' so designated before 1865 to distinguish them from slaves.

> ...The Virginia Bureau of Vital Statistics...has made a study by groups and families of the principal borderline aspirants for racial change. The chief sources of information are the early birth and death records, made by tax assessors from 1853 to 1896; marriage records from 1853 to date; United States Census reports for 1830, 1850, and 1870...

> Public records in the Office of the Bureau of Vital Statistics and in the State Library, indicate that there does not exist today a descendent of Virginia ancestors claiming to be an Indian who is unmixed with negro blood. Since our more complete investigation of all of these records and the statements (mostly signed) of numerous trustworthy old citizens, many now dead, all preserved in our 'racial integrity' files, no one has attempted by early recorded evidence to disprove this finding. If such evidence exists, our research worker would have found it.

Included with the copy of the letter that Peter Houck gave me was a copy of the list Plecker had supplied to clerks and registrars all over Virginia. This particular list was for Rockbridge and Amherst counties. If a surname appeared on the list all people with that name were to be recorded as "negroe" on all official documents. In essence Plecker was instructing clerks and registrars to ignore all other evidence and classify people according to his proclamation. The list for Rockbridge and Amherst contains twenty-nine family names. Peter Houck has referred to it as "Plecker's Hit List." That is a fitting description.

But what of Plecker's historical "proof" of the racial background of these families? On August 26, 1987 *The Richmond News Leader* published an article on the treatment of Virginia's Indians during the 1920s. It included remarks made by Russell E. Booker Jr., the current Registrar of Vital Statistics in Virginia. Booker explained that in the nineteenth century the term "colored" had been used to designate any race other than Caucasian and that "colored" and "free" were terms often applied to people who were recognized to be Indians.

> In the mid-19th century, state records for births, marriages and deaths were divided into two categories: 'white' and 'colored.' The 'colored' category was subdivided into 'free' and 'slave.'
>
> 'In the 1920s, when Plecker and his friends got the racial integrity acts passed 'colored' had been defined as 'Negro',' Booker said. 'Indians, who had been considered 'colored,' now were considered to be black.'
>
> Plecker didn't stop after pushing race laws through the legislature. He went further.
>
> 'He could change records, and he did,' Booker said. If someone came in and said, 'I'm Indian,' Plecker could say, 'Your grandfather was free negro. So you're Negro.' Actually, the grandfather wasn't listed as 'Negro' at all, but as 'colored-free.'
>
> Plecker browbeat local registrars into changing records. He made a list of surnames of people who claimed to be Indian. He browbeat hospitals—'We know who these people are. *You* know who they are.' Hospitals learned not to record these family names as Indian.
>
> ...What this is, is documentary genocide.

Plecker's attempt at documentary genocide is nowhere more evident than in his effort to eliminate the Indian people of central Virginia, the "Mongrel Virginians." The Powell Collection at the University of Virginia contains numerous letters from Plecker to the Clerks of Amherst and neighboring Rockbridge and Augusta counties concerning these people. The letters contain both appeals for assistance in identifying the families to be denied registration as Indian or white and instructions as to the requirements of the race integrity laws. Other letters contain Plecker's arbitrary judgments concerning the race of people he had never seen and for whom he had no valid records. A July 1924 letter that Plecker sent to a descendent of the Amherst Indian group who have moved to Rockbridge County demonstrates the vehemence with which Plecker was approaching these people. It also illustrates how he attempted to intimidate them into complying with his judgement of their racial status. The letter was apparently written after the person Plecker is addressing had complained to the local registrar about the list of names that Plecker had requested. It is also important to note that Plecker claims in this letter to have knowledge of names from McDougle's and Estabrook's study. As I reported in the last chapter, in fact he did not.

Dear Sir:

Our local registrar, Miss Aileen Goodman...in her letter to us says that you want us to write to you at once regarding the question of sending us a list of the names of your people.

...I do not know you personally and have no positive assurance as to your racial standing but I do know that an investigation made some time ago by the Carnegie Foundation of the people of mixed descent in Amherst County found [your] family [name to be] one of those known to be mixed. We learned also that members of this family and of other mixed families have crossed over from Amherst County and are now living on Irish Creek.

The report of these families in book form will soon be published in which the various families are traced back to the beginning. It has been found that they are descendants in part from three Indians who mixed with white and negro people and that there are now about five hundred of such mixed type of people who cannot be claimed as pure white under the new law.

We will be very glad to have you and your family and others to register but want to assure you that it must be done correctly. We do not expect to be easy upon anyone who makes a misstatement and we expect soon to be in possession of facts which we can take into court if necessary.

...We trust that you will instruct the people of Irish Creek very clearly as to the law and of the fact that it is my duty to see that this law is properly enforced and that I expect to do it with absolute impartiality and without regard to how it may affect any individual person.

In the future no clerk in Virginia is permitted to issue a marriage licenses for the marriage of persons of mixed descent with white people and our Bureau expects to make it plain to clerks that this law must be absolutely enforced.

I will be glad to hear what you have to say and particularly to have the dates and places of the births and marriages of yourself, your parents and grandparents.

We have instructed physicians, local registrars and midwives to see that all persons of mixed descent in Amherst and Rockbridge Counties are correctly reported and that they be not reported as white. If any have done so in the past, the cards should be returned and the corrections made on the certificates.

We are also advising the school authorities that these people of mixed blood should not enter white schools.

Indeed Plecker's assault on what the Amherst group must surely have perceived as their own racial integrity had a disturbing effect on them. It also led them to take action. In an August 9 letter that same year Plecker described their reaction to his list making. He explained to his friend and colleague Ernest Cox that: "Our Amherst County colony is up in arms and are on the verge of a race riot, threatening the life of one of our local registrars for giving out information concerning them. About 47 from Irish Creek, Rockbridge county, who belong to the Amherst tribe sent in registration cards all white, though we know positively that most, if not all of them are mixed."

It appears that both the Johns and Sorrel court cases discussed previously were attempts to deliberately stop the uses to which the race integrity legislation and the offices of the State Registrar were being put against the Amherst Indians. After Judge Holt had ruled against Dorothy Johns and in favor of the Clerk who had refused to issue a licence for her marriage to a "white man," Plecker wrote letters to court clerks in both Amherst and Rockbridge expressing concern that another case was being prepared. He also expressed a need to know what information was being gathered from courthouse records and to what end. His letter of October 4 to the Clerk of the Amherst Circuit Court is telling of his anxiety over the plans of those he viewed as his adversaries.

> As you know, Hon. A. T. Shields, Clerk of Rockbridge County, refused to grant a marriage license to Dorothy Johns and a white man, and when they got out a mandamus to compel it...[I] appeared as [a] witness.
> I had all of the Amherst County birth records and we showed conclusively that she was descended from the Amherst family of Johns, all of whom are listed in the old records as of colored descent.
> It seems that their lawyer has persuaded them that their case is not finally settled, and that others of their tribe can secure recognition as white or Indian.
> ...I have been told by Hon. A. W. Robertson of Lexington, Commonwealth Attorney for Rockbridge County, that they are preparing a family tree and expect to contest it at the November Court. What I desire to know is if they have been securing any evidence from your old birth and death records, copies of which we have in our office? If so, give us any advice that you can as to the names they are tracing and the result of their findings.
> ...As this is a very important case, we should be prepared to meet every emergency.

Plecker sent a copy of this letter to the Rockbridge Clerk of Court and asked that he respect the same request. He warned the Clerk that the family in question was even more likely to make a search of his records because his office was more convenient to them and likely to be perceived as containing something that would be useful to them. He closed his letter by saying, "I especially desire that you post me as to everything in connection with the case and along just what lines they are working, as I am in complete ignorance as to anything except that they are preparing to spring some sort of surprise at the November Court."

The "surprise" in the Court in November was, of course, the Atha Sorrels case. As was discussed earlier, when Judge Holt rendered his decision in the Sorrels case he not only decided in favor of Atha Sorrels' right to marry a white man, he also challenged the rationality of the racial integrity law and the kind of evidence of race impurity which had been produced in the case. He found invalid the kind of records that Dr. Plecker had produced as evidence of race mixture. Given this judgement it is incredible to think that Plecker continued using just this kind of misinformation as the basis of his assault on the Amherst Indian people for two decades and more. Incredible, but that is exactly what he did.

For years Plecker pursued these people in an aggressive and hostile fashion. He not only denied them birth certificates and marriage licenses designating them as Indians, he changed their racial status on official records according to his own will and informed them by proclamation of what he had decided that their racial designation would be in the records of his office. The designation that he always made was, of course, "colored" or "negro."

Walter Plecker and his staff monitored documents being processed through his office from Amherst and surrounding counties carefully according to his list of "mixed" families. He consistently refused to process records for these families listing them as white or Indian and demanded that they comply with his judgments of their racial status. He often threatened them with penitentiary terms if they violated the race integrity statutes.

A 1939 case provides a good example of the stalking character of Plecker's search for the Indians he refused to allow to be Indians. Plecker wrote on May 15 to the Clerk of the Circuit Court of Bedford County concerning a man who had applied for a marriage license and about whom the Clerk had questions. I have deleted names of the people whose racial status was being questioned.

> We have your inquiry in reference to the racial status of _____, who appears to be of mixed blood but who made application to marry a white girl.
>
> We do not know whether we can establish his racial descent until we have had further information as to his family. We are sending two questionnaires one for _____ and the other for _____. They should answer all of the questions if possible. In many of these cases illegitimacy figures, and if they are not able to give the full pedigree for that reason, this is good cause for suspicion.
>
> ...There is a large group of mixed _____ in Amherst and Rockbridge Counties. Is it possible that he has worked his way to Roanoke County [where the applicant had listed his residence]? All of the _____ of Amherst County are mixed.
>
> If this young man has the appearance of being a mulatto and cannot prove the contrary, I would suggest that no license be granted to him. However, the chances are that they will slip over into an adjoining county and get a license by giving false information.

It is important to note that this letter demonstrates that Plecker's tactics had remained the same. He had no problem with a racial judgement being made solely on the basis of appearance and the burden of proof was placed on the person whose race was being questioned rather than on the questioner. The fact that both approaches had been found to be legally unsound by Judge Holt in 1924 seems to have been of no significance to Plecker. He continued to operate on these bases and they worked for him. People were intimidated and their lives substantially altered by his arbitrary judgments and decrees.

Plecker's vigilance in the case of the young man applying for a marriage license in Bedford County yielded results. A few days later he, or a member of his staff, noticed a marriage license had been issued this same man in a neighboring county. In a May 17 letter to the Clerk of Roanoke County he expressed disapproval, asked for more information, and suggested conditions that might lead to charges being brought against the couple.

> We learn with regret that a license was issued in your office for the marriage of _____, age 21 and _____, age 16.
>
> Mr. Nichols, the Clerk of Bedford County, tells us that the mother of this man was ____. Since Mr. Nichols describes him as apparently of mixed blood, we presume he belongs to the Amherst- Rockbridge group...Did you or your deputy, whichever issued the license, observe the same characteristics?
>
> As we have no positive information as to the man's pedigree, we can only surmise it from Mr. Nichols' observation as to his appearance. Shall this man, if he is of the Amherst group, be turned loose upon the community to raise more mulatto children?
>
> We inferred from Mr. Nichols' letter that the bride was a resident of Bedford County. What statement did she make on her marriage application? If she claimed to be a resident of Roanoke County to you and of Bedford County to Mr. Nichols, she has falsified in one case or the other...

Dr. Plecker was so immersed in his mission to destroy the claims of the Amherst group to Indian heritage that at least on one occasion he felt compelled to threaten a local government official. In 1940 he wrote to the Clerk of the Circuit Court in Rockbridge County expressing his unhappiness over a birth certificate which had been issued to a newborn of the Amherst group.

> I am amazed that you would register one of these Amherst negroes as white. It certainly cannot be because you do not know that all of the Amherst _____ are negroid...Somebody has made himself liable to the penitentiary for registering a negro as white as you will note in Section 5099a, Paragraph 2 of the Virginia Code. Just who it is and how many is for you and _____ between you to decide.
>
> If you will fill out a birth certificate giving the race as colored and send it in with your attestation...we will accept it, but not as white...
>
> I am holding the certificate as evidence...

Walter Plecker's campaign against the Amherst Indian people continued unimpeded for many years. He seemingly wielded his authority most effectively, and intimidated and manipulated the people who were his targets. There was little official protest and no public action on their part. Perhaps they had come to believe that any public exposure only made them more vulnerable to harm. Whatever the case, they suffered these abuses largely in silence. In contrast to their silence Plecker became more bold and aggressive in his actions against them. Now, in addition to controlling the race designation on the birth certificates and marriage licenses of the Amherst group, he began to go back and alter records that had been established before he began his racial crusade into their lives. A common practice for him became the adding of what he claimed was an accurate racial history on the backs of birth certificates which had earlier been issued listing the person as Indian or white. These notations consistently listed the heritage of the individual as "colored" or "negro" and indicated that the race claimed on the front of the certificate was inaccurate. Letters in the Powell Collection show that Plecker repeatedly refused to remove these notations from birth records and that he insisted that his racial information on these people was accurate.

A pause in Plecker's campaign was created, however, by an incident which caused an official examination of his techniques and the substance of his claims. It also provides a revealing glimpse at the realities of his methods. The incident was precipitated by a 1942 letter from William Kinkle Allen requesting birth certificates for several people in the Amherst Indian group. Mr. Allen also apparently asked that no notation be placed on the copies of the original certificates that he was requesting. Plecker's September 23 reply was characteristic of responses he had given to similar requests in the past.

> Replying to your request of September 10th, we are sending you a photostat copy of the certificate of birth of _____, said...to have been born June 9, 1919...As the race is incorrectly stated [on the certificate], we will not issue a certificate without a note on the back showing that it is not accepted for record for race as written. The note shows the additional information secured from the U.S. Military Records made by the U.S. Army of Occupation after the War Between the States.
>
> In that list the great-grandfather of _____ gave his race as colored and that is shown on all of the records in the line of descent. We will not change the race of this family from that shown in the early records and as shown by the great-grandfather himself.
>
> The Racial Integrity Act of 1924 places upon the State Registrar the responsibility of correctly classifying the population of the State by race in the Vital Statistics Records of the Bureau of Vital Statistics.
>
> The births of _____ on July 24, 1906 and of _____ on January 24, 1911 occurred before the present Vital Statistics law became effective and can be registered only as delayed birth certificates on the special form...enclosed, with sufficient evidence furnished as to the correctness of date. Of course, we will accept nothing except colored on these certificates.

I am certain that Plecker felt that this was the end of the matter and that, as in other cases of this kind, he would hear nothing more from Mr. William Kinkle Allen. He was mistaken. Allen's next move was to initiate action on behalf of two other people from the Amherst group who had earlier been told by Plecker that their birth certificates would always include the racial origin notation that he had decided was correct. On October 1, 1942 Plecker received a letter from John Randolph Tucker, an attorney with a prestigious Richmond law firm.

> My dear Sir:
>
> At the request of Mr. Wm. Kinkle Allen, of Amherst, Virginia, we hereby make application for a copy of the birth certificate of _____, born October 31, 1917, in Amherst County, Virginia...and the birth certificate of _____, born August 20, 1922 in Amherst County, Virginia...

Some time ago application was made direct to you by these parties for copies of the record in your office which was furnished under the following certification:

'I hereby certify that the above is a true and correct reproduction of the original certificate on file in the State Bureau of Vital Statistics, Richmond, Virginia

Jan. 10, 1942   W. A. Plecker
                       State Registrar'

On the back of these certificates appears the following:

'The Virginia Bureau of Vital Statistics does not accept the racial classification 'Indian' on this certificate as correct and does not admit the correctness of that term for the race of the parents of _____and, the parents of _____, were married on Feb. 1, 1916, in Amherst County, Virginia under a colored license. Furthermore, the grandparents and great-grandparents are colored and descendants of free negroes. Under the law of Virginia, _____ is, therefore, classified as a colored person.

                       W. A. Plecker
                       State Registrar'

Tucker continued his letter stating:

Section 1580 of the Code requires the State Registrar, upon request, to furnish any applicant a certified copy of the record of any birth registered under the provisions of the Act. I find no where in the law any provision which authorizes the Registrar to constitute himself judge and jury for the purpose of determining the race of a child born and authorizing him to alter the record as filed in his office by the local registrars. I desire and demand a correct copy of the record in your office as it there appears, without comment from you and without additions or subtractions, and I hereby notify you that unless I obtain a prompt compliance with your official duties, as prescribed by law, I shall apply to a proper court for a mandamus to compel you to perform your duty as prescribed by the statute.

For your own information, and as a matter of fairness, however, I desire to say that your statement that _____ and _____, parents of these children, were married in February 1916 under a colored license is not supported by the record. I have before me a certified copy of this marriage license in which the race of the parents is stated as 'white.' In this marriage license the names of the parents of the husband...are stated... I have also before me a certified copy of the marriage certificate of these people in which their race is shown to be white. It would seem, therefore, that in this particular instance, not only have you gone beyond your duties as prescribed by law, but that the notation which you have placed on the back of these birth certificates is contrary to the facts, as shown by the official records in Amherst County.

I trust that you will be good enough to let me have the requested certificates promptly.

Plecker quickly began to prepare himself to do battle with Mr. Tucker over this matter. He wrote to the Clerk of the Amherst Circuit Court, William Sandidge, explaining the situation and asking for his help with the matter. In particular he asked for help with the discrepancy between the marriage license he claimed listed the parents as colored and that Tucker asserted listed them as white. Plecker seemed confident, however, that things would be resolved to his satisfaction and stated that he planned to consult the Attorney General and would withhold the certificates upon the conditions demanded by Tucker if given the legal advice to do so. He closed his October 6 letter to Sandidge with an even more confident statement. "We can doubtless find much other documentary evidence, however, substantiating the fact that this family is of colored descent. We have not as yet taken the time for the research work required."

I cannot imagine that Walter Plecker could have been in any way prepared for the shock of the letter William Sandidge wrote to him the very next day. He was to discover in this letter that the only documentation he had for his racial claims in the case was unreliable. On the occasion of the first serious challenge to his authority on such matters in nearly two decades, he was to be without any supporting evidence. What might have been criticized as weak evidence in fact proved to be nonexistent evidence. The circumstances described in Sandidge's letter are unusual. I find them, in fact, to be incredible but I will leave it to you, the reader, to make your own assessment.

Dear Dr. Plecker:

I have today referred to marriage register No. 4, and find that the classification as to race or color is plainly stated as 'Indian' where the record of this marriage is entered. However when I referred to the [actual] marriage license issued to _____ and _____ on Jan. 31, 1916, I find that the race on same has been altered, the license was filled in on a typewriter and the original entry under race has been erased and the word 'white' has been inserted with pen and ink. A certified copy of this marriage license was made several weeks ago and the office assistant making same did not think it important to call my attention to the alteration, if I had known that this alteration existed at the time the copy was made and certified I would have so noted same on the copy.

If I can be of further assistance to you in this matter or in any other please call on me.

With highest regards, I am
William Sandidge, Clerk

Plecker must have recognized immediately that he was defeated in this case, that he simply had no legal or documentary legs to stand on. He did, as he had originally told Sandidge he was going to do, consult the Attorney General but not with the results he had anticipated. Apparently on the same day he received Sandidge's letter, October 8, he wrote to J. R. Tucker sending him copies of the birth certificates. They were, as they had been requested, free of notations on the back. His letter to Tucker was filled, however, with resentment and bitter warnings.

Dear Sir:

I received your letter of October 1, 'demanding' photostat copies of the certificate of birth of _____ and _____ , who were said by midwives, members of the 'free issue' group, to be Indians.

As you point out, and as the Attorney General advises, the law does not permit us to give the truth on the certificates but seems to compel me as State Registrar to certify to what I know to be absolutely false. I regret that you put the matter upon the basis of this legal defect rather than upon the question of the race of this family. Of all of the families of the 'free issue' group of Amherst county, there is none perhaps that is more certainly and positively of negro descent than the _____ family. This fact can be established by many forms of documentary evidence...

Possibly you do not realize the seriousness of the matter in which you are taking part. Our apparent helplessness in giving information is one of the serious situations that comes from this small defect in the law. The purpose of these people is not simply, if possible, to establish their claim that they are Indians but to use that means of entering and marrying into the white race, which they can do if they claim vociferously and for a sufficient length of time that they are Indian with no negro admixture.

The second point which you make, which concerns me almost as much as what I have referred to above, is the fact that you have a certified copy of the marriage license of the parents of these children in which their race is stated as white, while the record as furnished to us by the same Clerk states that they are colored—the source from which our statement that they married under a colored license was taken...I immediately wrote to Mr. Sandidge, the Clerk, for an explanation and am sending you a photostat copy of his reply, in which he admits that his record was altered. This was probably done by his deputy, as Mr. Sandidge has been one of the most valiant defenders of his county against the efforts of this group of negroids to force themselves into the white race. Some years ago representatives from our office met the county officials of Amherst County in a conference at Amherst Court House, in which we went over, name by name, the various families of 'free issues' who were trying to pass as white. Mr. Sandidge took part in that conference, in which all agreed that the _____ and _____ families, along with a number of other families, should be classed as negroes and not as white and not as Indian.

We are enclosing the photostat copies of the birth certificates.

Within a few days Plecker wrote to his old friend and colleague, John Powell, about this incident. After describing the circumstances and the outcome, which he characterized as the "worst backset which we have received since Judge Holt's decision," he talked about his strategy for changing his vulnerable position in this regard. He explained that he planned to try to have legislation introduced to the next General Assembly which would legitimize his practice of making racial notes on the backs of birth certificates. He then made a disclosure to Powell which is so telling of Plecker's methods and ethics. He admitted to Powell that, "In reality I have been doing a good deal of bluffing, knowing all the while that it could not be legally sustained. This is the first time my hand has absolutely been called."

This setback, however, did not bring Walter Plecker's racial campaign against the Indians of Amherst to a halt. He was very quickly back to devising ways to force these people into the racial classification he had dictated that they were to have. In February of 1943 he corresponded with William Sandidge concerning a marriage license that Sandidge had processed with the designation for both parties as "Indian Mixed." He urged that in the future Sandidge should eliminate the word "Indian" from such licenses and leave just the word "mixed." He indicated that the word "colored," however, was still preferred if he could find a way to use it. He asked Sandidge to authorize him to change the license in question from "Indian Mixed" to "Colored." In other words he was suggesting that would make that change in his office and leave the people that had been registered as Indian in Sandidge's office unaware of that change. He also reiterated a plea for cooperation from Sandidge in putting down this "Indian falsehood." Plecker issued similar pleas to other local registrars, physicians, and other people of power and influence in the region surrounding Amherst County.

By February of 1944 Plecker had successfully prevailed upon the political influence of his powerful friends in Richmond. On February 22 the General Assembly approved an act amending the Code of Virginia relating to the State Registrar of Vital Statistics. Included in the provision of that amendment was the following statement:

> Whenever the State Registrar is requested to furnish a certified copy of a birth, death, or marriage certificate of a person and the records in his office or other public records concerning such person or his or her parents or forebears are such as to cause the Registrar to doubt the correctness of the racial designation or designations contained in the certificate, copy of which is requested, it shall be the duty of the State Registrar to enter upon the backs of the original certificate and certified copy an abstract of such other certificates or records, showing their contents so far as they are material in determining the true race of the person or persons named in the original certificate and the certified copy, with special reference to the records, indicating where same are to be found open to public inspection.

Walter Plecker had won again. The Indians of Amherst, Virginia and human dignity had lost. Although Walter Plecker would soon retire and the vengeance of his genocidal efforts would subside, the effects of the laws which were the foundation of his work did not. The laws and practices they supported remained in effect until 1967. It was in that year that the Supreme Court of the United States ruled that Virginia's Racial Integrity Act of 1924 and miscegenation laws in other states were unconstitutional. The Court found that such laws were not defensible on any legal or scientific basis. The major legal foundation for more than forty years of harassment of the Amherst Indians was dismantled. The harassment continued, however, and continues today. When and if it dies, prejudice dies slowly. Many people in the Central Virginia region still speak with cynicism and disdain of these people and their Indian heritage. Many who may be well intentioned but are misinformed refer to them as "Issues" or "Ishys" as if these were benign, not racist, terms. The people who have suffered hurt and indignity for so long still struggle for cultural and psychological survival. Only recently have they begun to heal themselves.

Only now are they beginning to resurrect their heritage, and to speak proudly and in public of their cultural roots.

References

Acts of Assembly, (1944), Chapter 52, Section 1580, Paragraph C.

Green, Barbara, (1987), "Racial laws thinned ranks of Va. Indians," *The Richmond News Leader*, August 26, pp. 18–19.

Plecker, Walter A., (1924), May 15 letter to the Clerk of Bedford Circuit Court, John Powell Collection, Alderman Library, University of Virginia.

_____, (1924), May 17 letter to the Clerk of Roanoke County, John Powell Collection, Alderman Library, University of Virginia.

_____, (1924), July 29 letter to Irish Creek resident, John Powell Collection, Alderman Library, University of Virginia.

_____, (1924), August 9 letter to Earnest Cox, John Powell Collection, Alderman Library, University of Virginia.

_____, (1924), October 4 letter to the Clerk of Amherst Circuit Court, John Powell Collection, Alderman Library, University of Virginia.

_____, (1924), October 4 letter to the Clerk of Rockbridge Circuit Court, John Powell Collection, Alderman Library, University of Virginia.

_____, (1940), September 11 letter to the Clerk of Rockbridge Circuit Court, John Powell Collection, Alderman Library, University of Virginia.

_____, (1942), September 23 letter to William Kinkle Allen, John Powell Collection, Alderman Library, University of Virginia.

_____, (1942), October 6 letter to William Sandidge, John Powell Collection, Alderman Library, University of Virginia.

_____, (1942), October 8 letter to J. R. Tucker, John Powell Collection, Alderman Library, University of Virginia.

_____, (1942), October 13 letter to John Powell, John Powell Collection, Alderman Library, University of Virginia.

_____, (1943), February 3 letter to William Sandidge, John Powell Collection, Alderman Library, University of Virginia.

Plecker, Walter A., (1943), December letter to local registrars, clerks, and legislators, Bureau of Vital Statistics, Commonwealth of Virginia.

Sandidge, William, (1942), October 7 letter to Walter A. Plecker, John Powell Collection, Alderman Library, University of Virginia.

Tucker, John R., (1942), October 1 letter to Walter Plecker, John Powell Collection, Alderman Library, University of Virginia.

CHAPTER NINE:

The Monacan Indians of Virginia

In 1908 a young seminary student wrote an account of the Indian people he had worked with during the summer between graduating from the University of Virginia and the beginning of his seminary studies. His name was Arthur Gray and he was writing about his experience in helping to establish a mission for the Indian people of Amherst County. His account was published in the *Diocesan Journal* that same year. He began the article with what he believed was true of the history of these people.

In the latter part of the 18th century, and the early part of the 19th, the inhabitants of the Piedmont section of Virginia were accustomed to see small bands of Indians passing through their farms, or stopping at their springs for water. These were generally members of the Cherokee or allied tribes, who dwelt on the borders of North Carolina, Tennessee and Virginia and who were in the habit of making pilgrimages to Washington to see the 'Great White Father', their route passing through or near Lynchburg or Charlottesville. On one or more of these pilgrimages some members of the band dropped off in Amherst County...

They are known locally as 'Issues.' This name has clung to them from ante-bellum days. Negroes who were not slaves were called 'Free Issues' and these people, being neither whites nor slaves, were classed with the 'Free Issues.' They dislike the name very much and they call themselves 'Indian Men,' and 'Indian Women'...

Owing to the fact that they will not associate with the negroes and cannot associate with the whites, their education and religious training has been sadly neglected. It is only in late years that the county school board has established a special school for these people in a little 16 x 18 log school house, and then it is hard to get a competent teacher for them. A few of the older ones have picked up enough 'learnin' to read and write a little, and the few children who have attended the school regularly have progressed well.

During the summer of 1907 [another]...student of the Theological Seminary of Virginia...began missionary work among these people. The little 16 x 18 log school house was used for a church, and an average congregation numbered about 100 persons...

Miss Cornelia Packard came last January to do missionary work among these people. She goes about through the mountains, from cabin to cabin, reading and praying and teaching them the simple truths of the Gospel, and ministering to the needs of the poor and sick...

The greatest need of the mission has been supplied this summer in the erection of a churchly little chapel on a beautiful site which nature seems to have contributed for the purpose. It is a triangle of solid rock, formed by the public road crossing two streams just before they unite with enough soil for a clump of trees about the front, facing the road. St. Paul's Chapel, as it will be called, was built mostly by the help of church people within and without the State, but partly by subscriptions and work from the [people]...themselves. They have given about $150 in cash, which is a splendid offering considering their circumstances; besides over $100 in labor and hauling.

...The mission will combine with the county this session and erect a suitable school building...There are 150 children under 16 years of age, who are capable of taking a good education, some of them being especially bright...

The chapel will be consecrated in the autumn and at the same time there will be a class of 25 or 30 for confirmation.

Any who wish to contribute to the general expenses of this mission, or to obtain any further information, may communicate with

Arthur P. Gray, Jr.
Theological Seminary, Virginia

The idea that the Amherst Indians were of Cherokee origin had been of longstanding. As early as 1896 Edgar Whitehead had referred to a Cherokee heritage for these people in an article he wrote for *The Times* of Richmond, one of the state's major newspapers at the time. Entitled "Amherst County Indians," the article was a clear testament to the Indian heritage of the people by someone who knew them well. Whitehead was from an established and influential family from the area where the Indians lived.

In this county it is not generally known that we have had a settlement of Cherokee Indians for many years...

In that portion of the foothills of the Blue Ridge mountains in Amherst County, known as the Tobacco Row Mountain, Bear Mountain, Stinnet's Mountain and Paul's Mountain...a race of people exists today claiming to be Cherokee Indians, and not without satisfactory proof. The older part were typical Indians, of rich copper color, high cheek bones, long, straight black hair, tall and erect in form, stolid...but of as manly bearing as some of Buffalo Bill's best specimens. The original settlers came to the county at an early period. William Evans, a Cherokee Indian first resided, about the time of the Revolutionary War, on Buffalo River...His daughter Mollie Evans married one William Johns, an Indian...

About the year 1825 William Johns purchased of Landon Cabell, 500 acres of land on Bear Mountain, and on this tract...he built a humble dwelling... Here he lived and died, a worthy and peaceable citizen, following farming as a business, and raised a large family of sons and daughters...One of his sons, Tarleton Johns, married Eliza Redcross, a daughter of John Redcross, a well known Cherokee Indian, and by Billy Evans, Mallory Johns, William Johns, and John Redcross, this colony was started. Two of them, Wm. Johns and John Redcross were known to the writer...Previous to the late war, these people were isolated and practically shut out from contact and intercourse with the whites, who were land and slave owners, and they on the other hand held themselves above the slaves. In this way there seemed to be no place for them, and no provision for such a race as to schools as there is now, and to some extent they were cut off from church privileges. The State law forbid the assembling of colored people unless specially permitted by the county court, and under the control of the whites, who had to be present. Indignantly rejecting the idea that they had African blood and scorning the term of 'free niggers,' but earnestly to this day claiming to be pure Indians, they could not enter the white churches and disdained to worship with the slaves, they became for the time as they really were, a separate and distinct race and colony...It is greatly to their credit that under such peculiar circumstances they did not become a settlement of thieves and murderers and their colony a hiding place for fugitives from justice. Shut out and hidden in the little coves of Bear Mountain where hunting and fishing, gambling and drinking amongst the 'bucks' was the Sabbath amusement, without schools and a gospel, and where no 'Sabbath's heavenly light' ever came for 25 years, could anything else have been expected but heathenism? Strange as it may seem it was not the case...

...From...Wm. B. Johns, born the 19th of February, 1799...I have been enabled to get much information about their history...On a recent visit to him, while I noted down his answers to my questions in my memorandum book, I glanced at this man of ninety-seven years, and as he stood before me with his well-defined Indian color and features, erect in form, with his white locks hanging down to his shoulders, a venerable relic of the past, standing on the threshold of the 20th century, a representative of a race soon to be 'numbered with the things that were,' I was forcibly reminded of Campbell's 'Last Man':

> I saw a vision in my sleep
> That gave my spirit strength to sweep
> Adown the gulf of time,
> I saw the last of human mould
> That shall creation's death behold
> As Adam saw her prime.

Edgar Whitehead

In 1928 Bertha Pfister Wailes submitted a thesis as a candidate for a Master of Arts degree from the University of Virginia. The title of the thesis was "Backward Virginians: A Further Study of the Win Tribe." As the title suggests, the study is a revisit of Estabrook's and McDougle's study. Wailes was a graduate of Sweet Briar College and, while she does not indicate it in her study, she may have known both Estabrook and McDougle. She also lived on a farm on which some of the Indian people of Amherst worked as tenant farmers and she had personal contact with several families from that group. Not only was the title "Backward Virginians" an improvement over "Mongrel Virginians," her study was focused on the people as individual human beings and included a genuine sensitivity to their experiences and perspectives. Although Wailes acknowledged the work of Estabrook and McDougle and expressed appreciation for the assistance of W. A. Plecker, her's is a different kind of study. She described the poverty of many of the people and examined the various social problems that they were experiencing. She reiterated the idea that racial mixture leads to personal and social deficiencies. Still, her study was different.

> The purpose of this study is not to prove that either white, Indian or negro blood predominates, but to present a true picture of a backward group of people, and to bring out certain possible causative factors. My interest is not the question of their race mixture as an end in itself, but rather as a means in the production of certain physical characteristics which have set this people apart, and thus helped to produce the isolation which I believe to be responsible, partly at least, for their backwardness...

> That these people are backward no one disputes, that they have always been backward is known also, and that they will remain so always is the firm conviction of neighboring whites who accept the existence of the Wins as a necessary evil.

> 'I cannot understand why the 'Ishies' should be interesting to anyone. They are no account, and really half negro,' is expressive of the sentiment of the white community.

> These backward Virginians, termed the lowest in the state, are the object of this thesis. It may well be called a further study of the Wins, their habits and customs, but an explanation for their backwardness is here sought in terms other than race mixture.

After devoting more than eighty pages to describing the social, economic and health problems of the people, Bertha Wailes briefly explored possible corrective actions. Considering that she was writing in the shank of the eugenic movement in America, it is refreshing to find that she did not suggest measures of tighter and tighter social control. She did not suggest separation or segregation, or institutionalization or sterilization. Instead she suggested that the social and economic environment in which the people were living needed to be changed.

> The solution it seems is along economic lines. Long term leases, that safeguard both tenant and landlord might check their constant moving around with its attendant evils. Assistance into land ownership for those who so desire...might be an inducement to industry and thrift.

> The hope has been expressed that the interest and cooperation of some person of means might be enlisted who would purchase a tract of land, divide it into small holdings, and give them a chance to buy at long terms. A small cannery, too, was suggested...

> They are not to be despised, but pitied, and whether Indian, white, negro, or mixed they need understanding rather than condemnation. Unless more assistance is given their outlook for the future is indeed dark.

An article in *The Washington Post* on June 15, 1969, shows that the idea that the Indian people of Amherst County were of Cherokee origin had persisted up through that time. It also illustrates that although some things had changed for these people, prejudice, discrimination and misunderstanding continued to plague their lives.

William Sandidge's comments to the reporter who wrote the article give a different impression of them than the one conveyed by his correspondence with Walter Plecker. They also give a different view of the Indian people than had been conveyed by other officials before. The Clerk of the Amherst Circuit Court, who was now 65 years old, said that "The Indians have a good record. I'd say local authorities have had less trouble with them over the years than with the other two races." This reference to the "other two races" is interesting for a man who had worked for years in an official climate that denied that the Indians were a race of their own. Sandidge, of course, had maintained records in a bureaucratic structure and political climate that insisted there were only two races in Virginia. Sandidge explained that he had no choice. "The marriage licenses always said 'white' or 'colored' and the law was clear that if there is any ascertainable blood other than Caucasian, I must list the applicant as colored."

By 1969 the mission which had been established by Arthur Gray, Jr. was being led by John Haraughty, a 44-year-old captain in the Evangelical Army of the Episcopal Church. Previous missionaries at St. Paul's Mission had served to protect the Indian people from the world that surrounded them and tried to provide them with what that outside world denied them. In the little classrooms at the mission they provided the children the only education they would receive. Not until 1957 were public school teachers assigned to these classrooms. The missionaries also provided the Indian people with religious services, social activities and a sense of community. John Haraughty's mission with these people was to be quite different. In his 1969 interview with the reporter from *The Washington Post* he said, "Getting our children into the public schools, where they could meet other people and find acceptance, is making a wonderful difference. It's drawing them out of their shell. For the first time we have kids in high school and a few might go to college. The 20 youngsters in my church youth group probably have a higher number of above C grades than you'll find in any average group of 20 high school students." The schools of Amherst County were indeed no longer closed to these children by 1969 and county school buses were making it possible for them to have much that had been denied to them before. One fifteen-year-old who a few years earlier would have been unable to attend high school was an honor student and pitcher for the high school baseball team.

Throughout *The Washington Post* article there were references to the Cherokee origins of the people. Most of these references seem to go back to the report in *The Richmond Times* in 1896 and Edgar Whitehead's description of the heritage of the Amherst Indians. By the late 1960s apparently, many of the people themselves had come to believe that this was the source of their genealogy.

Peter Houck, however, in *Indian Island* traces the heritage of Amherst's Indians back to the Monacan division of the Sioux nation. The people who were the early inhabitants of the Indian settlement in Amherst County, people with the names of Johns, Evans, Redcross and Branham, had hereditary ties to people who had lived in the foothills of the Blue Ridge Mountains for thousands of years. The Monacan people who survived Plecker's attacks and

Estabrook's and McDougle's literary assassination, and those who still suffer indignities today, have a cultural history that extends back millennium upon millennium. This is the reality even though they were told so often and so harshly that they did not even exist as a race of people.

For over half of the twentieth century the Monacan people lived an isolated existence both physically and socially. They eked out a living, many earning most of their livelihood in nearby orchards, and they lived in the humble log homes described by Wailes in her thesis. Their children had only scarce educational opportunities and medical care was very limited.

Today the Monacans have largely escaped their literal isolation. They live and work throughout the Central Virginia region. Their children have opportunities that were denied their parents and grandparents. The scars of past discrimination and the fact of continuing prejudice is real and present, of course, but things are looking better. Perhaps they have survived the worst assault.

The Virginia Council on Indians voted at its May 1988 meeting to recommend that the Monacan tribe be recognized by the Commonwealth of Virginia. The Monacans have formalized their tribal structure and have a chief, two assistant chiefs and a tribal representative. Legislation was passed in the General Assembly in 1989 making the Monacans the eighth tribe to be officially recognized by the Commonwealth of Virginia.

Chief Ronnie Branham was interviewed by Barbara Green of *The Richmond News Leader* in 1987. Portions of that interview provide a good perspective on the current state of the Monacan people.

> Branham said the tribe has some 350 members now. Most of them live in an around Amherst and Nelson counties, Lynchburg and Bedford; some live as far away as New Jersey. While a handful of friendly whites have helped the Monacans from time to time over the years, he gives credit for the present-day survival of tribal unity to 'this place' and to John Haraughty.
>
> 'This place' is a plot of ground on the side of Bear Mountain where the tribe has its headquarters. The site of an Episcopal Church mission to the Indians since 1906, the headquarters complex contains a small white church, the tribe's original one-room schoolhouse, a cinder-block tribal center and other small buildings on foundations carved out of rock.
>
> It has a playground with swings and climbing apparatus. A bubbling creek spanned by wooden bridges winds its way through the sun-dappled clearing in the woods. On top of the mountain is a baseball field.
>
> John Haraughty is a Captain in the Church Army who has been leader of the mission since 1968...When he arrived, the tribe had no income and could offer no financial help. Now the tribe pays all expenses except a portion of his salary.
>
> 'He's been our unifying, motivating force,' said Branham. 'He's kind of like a godfather, I guess.'
>
> Under Haraughty's stewardship, the Monacans came out of their mountaintop isolation to seek medical care and modern housing. With his help, the tribe bought 200 acres...and built Orchard Hill Estates subdivision. It now

holds 28 homes and families...Branham and Haraughty were the first to move their families there in 1973.

The Orchard Hills Community Development Association, which built the subdivision, has plans to build a community center, craft shops and art galleries on tribal land. They will offer employment for tribe members.

The tribe also has the Orchard Hills Utilities Service, which owns two wells that furnish water to the subdivision homes.

...'You can't separate the church and the tribe,' says Haraughty, a white-haired Irishman from Oklahoma. 'They're all the same people.'

Branham also gives Haraughty credit for a bazaar and tribal reunion the Monacans have held the first Saturday in October for more than 15 years. From 9 in the morning till 9 at night, tribe members gather to talk, eat and meet relatives they may not have met before. Women of the tribe make quilts, canned goods, preserves and baskets to sell. The tribe serves a buffet lunch to 150 members and non-members alike.

...Haraughty, 63, will retire from the mission in two years. Before he goes, he hopes the diocese will agree to build a conference center on the mountain above Orchard Hill Estates, he said. When he goes the chaplain at Sweet Briar College will come to Bear Mountain on Sundays to conduct religious services.

'Then the tribe will pick up all the costs,' he said, 'and become a self-supporting parish.'

The Monacans have come a long way since the days when Branham, 42, a Vietnam veteran, had to join the U.S. Army to get a high school education. But it still has a long way to go. Asked for a wish list, Branham had to ponder for awhile to decide what to say first....'We've been deprived of so much. We were deprived of descent homes. We were deprived of an education. Some of the older ones can write their names and that's all.

'But if we could get decent homes for everybody, decent schools...

Of course, we would like to have all our land back. You asked for dreams.' Branham smiled. 'But we know better. They would have to give us half the state of Virginia back.'

On an October morning in 1988, while I was in midst of writing the first draft of this book, I attended the Monacan's Fall Bazaar at Saint Paul's Mission. My family and I had attended the Bazaar in previous years and we looked forward to the delicious and plentiful food at the buffet.

As we toured the displays of crafts, preserves and baked goods I felt that I noticed something different. There seemed to be a clear sense of pride being expressed for the Indian heritage of the people taking part in the bazaar. At one table there was information concerning the history of Virginia's Indians and a description of the Monacan's recognition by the Virginia Council of Indians. I overheard an elderly woman saying to a friend, "I wish the old ones who suffered so much could see this." She was referring to the Indian literature on the table and the obvious pride of Phyllis Hicks, the Monacan woman who was displaying it.

At another table there was a display of Indian crafts which had been made by people on the Pamunkey Reservation in King William County which is in the eastern region of Virginia. At that display I met Chief William Miles and his wife. They had brought the Pamunkey items to the bazaar at the request of the Monacan organization. We had a pleasant conversation and then my young children pulled me along to another exhibit.

After lunch I took a walk around the wooded lot where the Mission stands on its natural foundation of rock. Chief Miles and Chief Ronnie Branham of the Monacans were also outside enjoying the beautiful fall weather. We talked for a while about the struggle of Virginia's Indians for survival. I explained to these two men my interest in telling part of the story of that struggle. Both offered to help me. I then mentioned the name of Walter Plecker and I could see a visible physical reaction in both of them. It was clear that the name itself evoked a posture of defensiveness. For a moment I felt sorry that I had mentioned a name that would create such a reaction at such a happy event as the bazaar. The men, however, wanted to talk of Plecker and the damage he, and the ideas that compelled him, had done to their people. Chief Branham then asked a rhetorical question that has stuck in my mind since, "How can one man do so much harm to so many people who did nothing to deserve it?" Indeed, how?

In 1989 we once again visited the Bazaar. There was a new booth set up by a woman who had done an extensive genealogical study of one of the Monacan families. While talking with her my wife discovered that there was a distant connection between her mother's family and the Monacan people. During the ride back to Lynchburg my daughters and my son spoke excitedly of being related to the Monacan Indians. Even when we tempered their excitement by explaining that the connection was long ago and through the marriage of distant relatives, they continued to talk with pride of being kin to the Indians. They felt richer for the connection, I felt richer for their sense of pride.

References

Gray, Arthur P. Jr., (1908), "Mission work among some Cherokee remnants in Virginia," *Diocesan Journal*, Sept.–Oct., 1908.

Green, Barbara, (1987), "Monacans rebound from hard times," *Richmond News Leader*, August 27, pp. 26–28.

Houck, Peter W., (1984), *Indian Island in Amherst County*, Lynchburg, VA: Lynchburg Historical Research Co.

O'Neill, William J., (1969), "The Amherst Cherokee: Virginia's Lost Tribe," *The Washington Post*, Sunday, June 15.

Wailes, Bertha P., (1928), *Backward Virginians: A Further Study of the Win Tribe*, Thesis presented to the Academic Faculty of the University of Virginia in candidacy for the degree of Master of Arts.

Whitehead, Edgar, (1896), "Amherst County Indians," *The Times*, Richmond, Va., April 19.

CHAPTER TEN:

Eugenics As Genocide

In the October, 1988 issue of *Natural History* Jared Diamond provides an important perspective on the practice of genocide. In his article, entitled "In Black and White," he examines the extermination of the aborigines of Tasmania as an example of intentional, planned and government-sanctioned genocide. The island of Tasmania lies 200 miles off the coast of Australia. When Europeans first explored there in the 17th century there were approximately 5,000 hunter-gathering aborigines living on the island.

When European settlement of Tasmania occurred in the nineteenth century the slaughter of the aborigines commenced. Beginning around 1800 white settlers kidnapped Tasmanian children as laborers and Tasmanian women as sexual consorts. They killed men, trespassed on their hunting grounds, and cleared them off land which they then claimed as their own. One settler shot Tasmanians with a swivel gun loaded with nails. Martial law in 1828 authorized killing any Tasmanian on sight in settled areas. Soon a bounty was declared on the aborigines, five pounds for adults and two pounds for children caught alive. "Black catching" became big business. Finally a commission was established to consider proposals for what was defined as the "problem of the natives." Proposals included capture for sale as slaves, poisoning, and trapping and hunting them with dogs. The commission finally settled on continued bounties and the use of the mounted police for captures.

In 1830 a missionary was hired to take all the remaining Tasmanians to a small island thirty miles off Tasmania. Many died in route, about 200 finally reached Flinders Island. The aborigines did not thrive on that island. The government reduced expenditures for their support in the hope that they would die out. By 1869 only two women and one man remained alive. The man died that same year and the last woman survived until 1876.

Diamond observes that all societies have cultural sanctions against murder and that for genocide to occur these sanctions must somehow be superseded. The factors that invoke the overriding of these sanctions, according to Diamond, include the following:

> ..self-defense, revenge, manifest rights to land, and possessing the correct religion or race or political belief. These are the principles that fan

hatred and transform ordinary people into murderers. A further universal feature of genocide is an 'us/them' ethical code that views the victims as lower beings or animals to whom laws of human ethics don't apply. For instance, Nazis regarded Jews as lice; French settlers of Algeria referred to local Moslems as ratons (rats); Boers called Africans bobbejaan (baboons); educated northern Nigerians viewed Ibos as subhuman vermin...

Genocide is something that we usually attribute to "those awful Nazis." In fact, however, genocide is a practice that has occurred repeatedly, even among "nice" people like our own ancestors. Although the physical extermination of native Americans was never completed, it came close to reaching fruition. And genocide is not something that ceased after the atrocities of the Holocaust became known to the world. Diamond points out that since 1950 there have been almost twenty genocidal episodes. Two, in Cambodia and Pakistan, claimed more than a million victims each. A rational consideration of an irrational phenomenon like genocide quickly reveals that it is not something committed only by hideous people with demonic motivations. Give it just a moment's thought and it must be clear that not all of the people who contributed to the attempted extermination of Europe's Jews were drooling psychopaths. Just as in other genocidal campaigns, most of the people who ran the gas chambers and operated the crematoriums, and those who turned their heads and said nothing were "nice" people. How is it that "nice" people can commit or support genocide.

Erik Erikson attributes the capacity for indecent and inhuman acts by decent human beings to what he has termed "pseudospeciation." This is how he refers to the process of an "in" group defining an "out" group and deciding that its members are less than human. When it is believed that a certain group is not really human the normal standards of human conduct toward them no longer apply. They are less than human and may, therefore, even be killed without crime, sin, or guilt. Diamond gives a contemporary example of the kind of thinking that may have led to the pseudospeciation of the Tasmanian people. He cites a letter written in 1982 to a leading Australian newspaper, *The Bulletin*. The letter, written by a woman named Patricia Cobern, was a defense of the early white settlers on Tasmania and a denial that they had participated in genocide.

> ...In fact, wrote Ms. Cobern, the settlers were peace loving and of high moral character, while Tasmanians were treacherous, murderous, warlike, filthy, gluttonous, vermin infested, and disfigured by syphilis. Moreover, they took poor care of their infants, never bathed and had repulsive marriage customs. They died out because of all those poor health practices, plus a death wish and lack of religious beliefs. It was just a coincidence that, after thousands of years of existence, they happened to die out during a conflict with settlers. The only massacres were of settlers by Tasmanians, not vice versa. Besides, the settlers only armed themselves in self-defense, were unfamiliar with guns, and never shot more than forty-one Tasmanians at one time.

Russell Booker, State Registrar of Virginia, described what Walter Plecker was trying to do to Indians in Virginia and the way he attempted to do it as "documentary genocide." I agree with his conception and will apply it more broadly. I have come to believe that the eugenics movement in America was an attempt at genocide on several fronts. It is clear to me that once the trappings of well intentions and "its for their own good" rationales are removed, the eugenics movement was an attempt to eliminate the presence of certain races and classes of people from American society. In some cases this meant geno-cide by taking away reproductive capacity; sterilization leading to a dying out of the strain. In other cases it meant genocide by removing people from society and containing them in institutions. In other instances it meant attempting to send a race of people "back to Africa" and thereby eliminating them from America. In still other cases it took the form of attempting to eliminate a race of people, Native Americans, by legislating and bureaucratizing them out of existence. In each case it was the people in question who were made to be viewed as an inferior strain of humanity. Whether it was poor white people, black people, or Native Americans, they were made into pseudospecies. As a result, "nice" people participated in and supported the attempted genocide of these groups.

And yet there is another facet to the reality of genocide as a social phenomenon. Although "nice" people have taken part in it, other "nice" people have refused to take part or have actively resisted it on behalf of its victims. Why? What distinguishes the otherwise decent people who become genocidal in their thoughts and actions from those who do not? In their brilliant book, *The Altruistic Personality: Rescuers of Jews in Nazi Europe*, Samuel and Pearl Oliner provide important insights on this question.

The Oliners point out that the period of World War II brought new dimen-sions of evil to the world. Millions of defenseless civilians were killed in Poland, Russia, and Yugoslavia. Gypsies all over Europe were slaughtered. Jews, however, were the special target of the Nazi machinery of genocide. They were made a pseudospecies and six million were murdered—more than 60 percent of all the Jews living under Nazi occupation. Much attention has been given, as it must continue to be given, to those who committed the murders and those who stood knowingly by.

Samuel and Pearl Oliner, however, report in their book on those who at great personal risk to themselves and their families stood against the social tide and helped Jews. They refer to this group of people as the "rescuers." They set out to research the question of why non-Jews would choose this diver-gent path that could result in their own deaths and possibly death to their fami-lies. Their interest in understanding the rescuers, however, transcends the attempted extermination of the Jews. The Oliners explain:

> Our study was designed to provide an understanding of European rescuers of Jews during World War II, but its goal transcends this particular group or European historical moment. The world is filled with groups marked

for special cruelty. The Holocaust ushered in a new death technology, as awesome in its implications as nuclear technology. Whereas nuclear warfare threatens to turn all of us into ashes, Holocaust technology created a means whereby selected populations could be plucked out from among their neighbors and destroyed. The Holocaust thus points not only to the fragility of Jews but to the precariousness of any group that might have the misfortune of being so arbitrarily designated. If we are to live in a world free from the threat of Holocausts, we will need to create it. If we can understand some of the attributes that distinguished rescuers from others, perhaps we can deliberately cultivate them.

The Oliners have found that rescuers of the Jews were "ordinary" people. They report that those who hid, fed, cared for and transported Jews to save them from the Nazi atrocities were farmers, teachers, business people, factory workers, rich and poor, Protestants and Catholics. They were ordinary people who were not recognizable as heroes in their bearings or in their personal histories. What did distinguish them, however, was their connectedness to others in their lives; their relationships of care and commitment. As the Oliners explain:

> ...Their involvements with Jews grew out of the ways in which they ordinarily related to other people—their characteristic ways of feeling, their perceptions of who should be obeyed; the rules and examples of conduct they learned from parents, friends, and religious and political associates; and their routine ways of deciding what was wrong and right. They inform us that it is out of the quality of such routine human activities that the human spirit evolves and moral courage is born. They remind us that such courage is not only the province of the independent and the intellectually superior thinkers but that it is available to all through the virtues of connectedness, commitment, and the quality of relationships developed in ordinary human interactions.

And so the Oliners have found that moral heroism resides in people as an expression of the ways that they come to ordinarily view and interact with other people. Further, they have found evidence that this heroism seems to be born out of the "ordinary" structures of human society. It appears that the rescuers learned their sense of connectedness and commitment from their families, schools and neighbors. It is apparent that within the rescuers there was a chemistry of influence from family, school and community that made them different from the non-rescuers, that made them care.

The Oliners' research, of course, points to the importance of the family as the crucible for the learning of care. It appears that heroic lessons are in fact learned in the home in relation to how people should be regarded and treated. In this sense "ordinary" parents may teach "ordinary" children the extraordinary quality of moral heroism. The Oliners emphasize, however, that the teaching of caring and commitment is a community responsibility. They stress that the school is the single institution outside the family that reaches all children and, therefore, it must be seen as a conduit for teaching the kind of independence of thought and feeling that allows individuals to resist the tyranny of prejudice, separatism and genocidal impulse.

> Schools need to become caring institutions—institutions in which students, teachers, bus drivers, principals, and all others receive positive affirmation for kindness, empathy, and concern. Participants need opportunities to work and have fun together, develop intimacies, and share successes and pain. Students also need opportunities to consider broad universal principles that relate to justice and care in matters of public concern. Discussions should focus on the logic and values, implications and consequences of public actions, as well as the philosophical heritage that underlies these principles. In short, caring schools will acknowledge diversity on the road to moral concern. They will invoke emotion and intellect in service of responsibility and caring.

In *Celebrations of Life*, René Dubos speaks of finding "local solutions to global problems." Although I became uncomfortable recently when I saw the phrase on a bumper sticker, I use as the title for a lecture I give each year to college and graduate students his challenge that we should "think globally but act locally." The meaning that he conveys through that phrase is that it is important that we be aware of and concerned about global problems but that the work needed to confront these problems usually must be done close to home, at the local level. The best place to start to contribute to the well-being of humanity and of our planet is in our own communities. Martin Luther King, Jr. changed the world but he started with a protest against discriminatory seating policies by a local bus company in Montgomery, Alabama. Ghandi, as well, changed the world by beginning with acts of seemingly little global significance such as a boycott on salt.

I have come to believe that the moral strength that we need in order to avoid involvement in or acquiescence to genocide in all its forms, physical, social, and psychological, must come from "local" sources, families, schools and communities. It must in a sense flow from the "bottom up" not from the "top down." We must depend upon these "local" institutions to educate the larger culture of its moral and ethical responsibilities. In this sense it is true that you cannot "legislate morality" or rely on moral excellence to be created by political leaders. On the contrary, only a morally educated citizenry can require and constitute a decent, just and compassionate government.

By examining the stories of eugenics and genocide contained in this book I have been made more sensitive to the need to work toward freeing our children (and ourselves) from the race and class stereotypes, and the fears they have generated, that have so long plagued humanity. Race and class prejudice (even in the name of science) is as demeaning to those who possess it as it is destructive to those toward whom it is directed. Is it not time that we "act locally" to liberate ourselves and our children from these life diminishing influences? Can we live with ourselves in peace if we do not try?

References

Diamond, Jared, (1988), "In black and white," *Natural History*, October, 1988, pp. 8, 10,12, 14.

Dubos, René, (1981), *Celebrations of Life*, New York: McGraw-Hill.

Oliner, Samuel and Oliner, Pearl, (1988), *The Altruistic Personality: Rescuers of Jews in Nazi Europe*, New York: The Free Press.

INDEX

Allen, William Kinkle, 95
altruistic personality, 111–113
Amherst-Rockbridge Indian Group, 77, 83–88, 89–108
Anderson, R.N., 63
Anglo-Saxon Clubs of America, 17–20, 23–34, 37–51, 75, 78
Armstrong, Samuel Chapman, 37
Aunt Celie, ix–xiv

Banks, John, 55
Banks, Lydia, 55
Bazile, Leon, 75
Booker, Russell, 90, 111
Branham, Ronnie, 106, 108
Brockenbrough, Elizabeth, 54
Brockenbrough, Rebecca, 54
Buchanan, Annabel, 47–49
Buck, Carrie, 4–6, 9–10, 83
Buck, Vivian, 6
Burleigh, Louise, 33, 52–55

Chickahominy Indians, 76–77
Cobern, Patricia, 110
Copeland, Walter Scott, 37–41
Cox, Earnest Sevier, 13–18, 23–24, 27, 52–54, 91
Cronon, Edmond, 23–24

Dabney, Thomas, 28
Darling, Frank, 45
Davenport, Charles, 79–80, 83, 86–88
Diamond, Jared, 109–110
DuBois, W.E.B., 39–40, 43–44
Dubos, Rene, 113

Edmunds, Pocahontas Wright, 20, 55
Erikson, Erik, 110
Estabrook, Arthur, 83–88, 91, 103, 106
eugenics, 2–11, 54, 79, 83–88, 111
Eugenics Record Office, 79, 83–88

Ferguson, Homer, 45

Galton, Francis, 2
Garvey, Marcus, 23–34, 40, 47, 49, 78
genocide, 109–113
Goddard, Henry, 3, 10
Gould, Stephen Jay, 13
Gray, Arthur, 101–102, 105
Green, Barbara, 106
Gregg, James E., 38–46
Guy, Henley, 38, 40, 47

Hampton Institute, 37–48
Haraughty, John, 105–107
Harrower, D.E., 76–77
Hicks, Phyllis, 107
Hofmann, Otto, 8–11
Holmes, S. J., 6
Holmes, Oliver Wendell, 5
Holt, Harry, 45
Holt, Henry, 71–75, 92–93, 98
Houck, Peter, 89–90, 105
Howard, John Tasker, 21

James, Arthur W., 51–54
Johns, Dorothy, 71–72, 74, 77, 92

Kallikak, Deborah, 3
Kallikak family, 3–5, 10

Laughlin, Harry, 6, 10
Ludmerer, K. M., 6

McDougle, I.E., 83–87, 91, 103, 106
McGuire, Stuart, 50–51
Mallison, George, 45
Mann, Abby, 7–8
Massenberg Bill, 40, 42–47
Massenberg, George, 40
Miles, William, 107–108
Monacan Indians, 77, 83–88, 89–100, 101–108
Munford, Mary Branch, 42–43

N.A.A.C.P., 27–28, 39, 42
Native Americans, 71–81, 83–88, 89–100, 101–108
Nazi war crimes, 6–11, 54, 81, 111–113
Nelson, Ray, 4
Nuremberg Military Tribunals, 8–10

Oliner, Pearl, 111–113
Oliner, Samuel, 111–113
"ordinary people, 112

Pamunkey Indians, 77, 107–108
Peel, Alfreda, 50
Peel, George, 50
Plecker, Walter Ashby, 34, 51–52, 59–70, 71–81, 83–88, 89–99, 103, 105
"poor white trash", 10
Popenoe, Paul, 6
Powell, John, 16–21, 23–34, 37–57, 59–60, 62, 69–70, 73–75, 78, 98
prejudice, xiii–xiv
pseudospeciation, 110

Racial integrity, 19–21
Race Integrity Law, 20–21, 59, 74, 86
Rafter, Nicole Hahn, 10

Rappahannock Indians, 77
rescuers, 111–113
Robinson, Caleb, 31–34

Sandidge, William, 96–99, 104–105
Sherman, Richard, 38
Shiuhushu, 78
Simms, L. Moody, 21
Smallwood, John, 31–32
social Darwinism, 2
Sorrels, Atha, 71–77, 92
Spencer, Herbert, 1–2
St. James, R.F., 78–80
Stagg, Flying Eagle, 78
sterilization, 4–11, 83
Strong Wolfe, Joseph, 78
Sweet Briar College, 83, 85, 103

Taft, William Howard, 43
Taylor, Carol, 39–40
Temperance Industrial and Collegiate Institute, 31–34
Thomson, Brian, 76
Thompson, Louise A., 44–45
Tovey, Donald Francis, 21
Tucker, John Randolph, 95–98

United Negro Improvement Association, 23–34, 47, 78

Virginia Indians, 71–81, 83–88, 89–100, 101–108

Wailes, Bertha Pfister, 103–104, 106
Whitehead, Edgar, 102–103, 105
Williams, Reid, 63
Wilson, May, 76
Winn, Ray, 76